Books in This Series

Closer Walk: 365 Devotions That Nurture a Heart for God

*Your Daily Walk: 365 Daily Devotions to Read
Through the Bible in a Year*

Family Walk: 52 Weekly Devotions for Your Family

*YouthWalk: Sex, Parents, Popularity,
and Other Topics for Teen Survival*

*YouthWalk 2: Commitment, Stress, Forgiveness,
and Other Topics for Teen Survival*

executive editor **bruce h. wilkinson**

author of *the prayer of jabez*

We want to hear from you. Please send your comments about this book to us in care of the address below. Thank you.

ZONDERVAN™

YouthWalk 2
Copyright © 2003 by Walk Thru the Bible

Requests for information should be addressed to:

Zondervan, *Grand Rapids, Michigan 49530*

or

Walk Thru the Bible
4201 North Peachtree Road
Atlanta, GA 30341

Library of Congress Cataloging-in-Publication Data

YouthWalk 2 : commitment, stress, forgiveness, and other topics for
teen survival / Bruce Wilkinson, executive editor ; Len Woods, editor ;
Paula A. Kirk, general editor.
    p. cm.
    Summary: A collection of daily devotionals designed to help the reader
understand the Bible and to provide practical ways of applying biblical teachings
to common problems and concerns.
    ISBN 0-310-24682-2
    1. Teenagers—Prayer-books and devotions—English. [1. Prayer books
and devotions. 2. Conduct of life—Biblical teaching.] I. Title: Youthwalk two.
II. Wilkinson, Bruce. III. Woods, Len. IV. Kirk, Paula.
    BV4850 .Y684   2003
    242'.63—dc21   2002013606

Interior design by Sherri L. Hoffman

Printed in the United States of America

---

02 03 04 05 06 07 08 /❖ DC/ 10 9 8 7 6 5 4 3 2 1

Dedication

When Christ gathered his disciples on the eve of his own greatest hour of testing, he revealed two great characteristics that he desired from his followers—servanthood and fruitfulness. With a rare blend, Nancy DeMoss is an outstanding example of a person who serves the Lord with deep commitment to bearing fruit that lasts for eternity. Nancy DeMoss and her like-minded family have borne much fruit, fruit that has remained. Yet they have done so as servants, hardly noticed, and sometimes not even known by those who are the beneficiaries. With great appreciation for her commitment, wisdom, and single-minded dedication to the cause of Christ, we lovingly dedicate *YouthWalk 2* to Nancy DeMoss.

Bruce H. Wilkinson

Contents

Real Life —•

Seeking Reality —•

Word Power —•

Viewpoint —•

Acknowledgments

YouthWalk 2: Commitment, Stress, Forgiveness, and Other Topics for Teen Survival is the second compilation of topical studies from *YouthWalk,* a magazine for teens published monthly by Walk Thru the Bible Ministries. We thank the many folks who have helped us out over the years, especially all the teens, youth leaders, and even parents who made up our focus groups, posed for photos, and wrote articles and letters that kept us on track. And we're especially grateful to all the people in Walk Thru the Bible's Specialized Publishing Group, from the leadership team to the staff in production.

Our *YouthWalk* design and production teams have invested their time and talents to produce material that will make a lasting difference in the lives of students. From start to finish their concern and prayers have been for those who will read *YouthWalk.* Our special thanks go to all of them for their creative ideas and their perseverance over the years.

Walk Thru the Bible

Walk Thru the Bible is an international Christian educational organization that contributes to spiritual growth worldwide through innovative Bible teaching in publications, seminars, and videos. Walk Thru the Bible has taught more people the life-changing truths than any other Bible seminar organization, hosting millions of participants in its live Bible seminars since 1976. Presenting biblical content in an easy-to-understand and memorable format, Walk Thru the Bible's video curriculum, devotional publications, and seminars equip millions each year to read and study the Bible.

What started as a vision to teach the Bible in a new way, fostering retention and understanding, has expanded into a worldwide movement. In the early 1970s Bruce Wilkinson developed *Walk Thru the Old Testament* and *Walk Thru the New Testament* seminars as an innovative way to teach an overview or survey of the Bible. By enabling people to actively participate in the learning process through memorable hand signs, the Word of God came alive and lives were changed. Bruce trained several friends to present the seminar in churches and the demand for this teaching grew quickly, leading to the formation of the organization that today has thousands of instructors around the world.

Walk Thru the Bible has four major outreaches including: Seminars, Publications, LifeChange Video, and International. The seminars today include the original Bible surveys and many additional series including: *A Biblical Portrait of Marriage, Understanding the Love of Your Life, Solving the People Puzzle, Seven Laws of the Learner, Teaching with Style, The Prayer of Jabez, The Secrets of the Vine,* and many others.

The printing of the first *Daily Walk* in 1978 launched Walk Thru the Bible's publishing ministry. *Daily Walk* is a monthly publication that helps people understand their Bible while reading it through in one year. *Daily Walk* is one of several devotional magazines published by the organization including: *Closer Walk, Family Walk, YouthWalk, Quiet Walk, Tapestry,* and *Indeed.*

The vision of Walk Thru the Bible's international program is to train, equip, and sustain one qualified Bible teacher for every population group of 50,000 in the world. This bold program has expanded into country after country as Christian leaders of each region are trained for this teaching ministry. As a result, millions of people receive Bible training each year throughout the world.

LifeChange Video distributes innovative Bible instruction from several major teachers including: Bruce Wilkinson, Howard Hendricks, Chip Ingram, and Ronald Blue. Titles include *The Seven Laws of the Teacher, Experiencing Spiritual Breakthroughs, Holy Ambition, The Vision of the Leader, Mastering Your Money, A Biblical Portrait of Marriage,* and *Personal Holiness in Times of Temptation.* Each video series is designed for group use with leader's guides and student workbooks to guide the discussion.

By focusing on the central themes of Scripture and their practical application to life, Walk Thru the Bible enjoys wide acceptance in denominations and fellowships around the world. In addition, it has carefully initiated strategic ministry alliances with many Christian organizations and missions of wide diversity and backgrounds.

From the first seminar to the latest product, the goal of Walk Thru the Bible is always to teach the Word to the world for lasting lifechange, in this generation, for the glory of God.

For more information visit our website at *www.walkthru.org* or contact us at the following address:

Walk Thru the Bible
4201 North Peachtree Road
Atlanta, GA 30341-1207
770-458-9300

A Letter to the Reader

Dear Reader,

As a Christian teenager, are you sometimes confused by our world? Do you ever feel pressure to do things you know you shouldn't? Have you ever been asked a tough question about Christianity—and not known the answer? Are you ever embarrassed about sharing your faith?

If you answered any of those questions with a yes, I've got good news for you: You're not alone. But the book you have in your hand can help!

Youth Walk 2 is carefully designed to help you understand the Bible and apply its truth to your life. *Youth Walk 2* will help you establish the Bible as your rock—your sure foundation in this unsure world. No longer will you see the Bible as a book of boring stories about things that happened eons ago. Instead, you'll see the Bible as *relevant*—a vital resource for you to live a happy, successful, and productive life.

We at Walk Thru the Bible are thrilled to join with Zondervan to make this Bible-reading guide available to you.

Bruce H. Wilkinson
Executive Editor

How to Get the Most Out of YouthWalk 2

Youth Walk 2 gives you six months of devotions, arranged by topics. You can start with the first topic or just jump in at any point in the book. Just circle the page numbers to mark which devos you've done.

Each devotional topic has an introductory page (to preview the topic) and five devotional pages (one for each weekday—Monday through Friday). Each of the daily devotional pages includes the following five sections:

1. *The Opening Story*—sets up the problem

2. *Look It Up*—shows what the Bible says about the problem

3. *Think It Through*—stimulates your thinking about the problem

4. *Work It Out*—gives practical suggestions for solving the problem

5. *Nail It Down*—shares other passages where you can find more wise counsel about the problem

But that's not all! In addition to the weekly devotional topics, *Youth Walk 2* will educate, stimulate, and motivate you with these exciting features:

- *Real Life*—Each of these pages gives biblical answers to an important current issue.

- *Seeking Reality*—These pages are stories of humankind's ultimate search: a relationship with God through Jesus Christ.

- *Word Power*—These fun-filled pages are full of little-known facts about God's Word.

- *Viewpoint*—The editors share their perspectives on sometimes controversial topics.

Do you want to do great things for God? Of course you do, or you wouldn't be reading this book. Follow the above instructions, and six months from now, you'll know God's Word better than you do today.

And that will be a great thing!

 topic

Self-control

mastering your desires

Seems like the same old story. You tell yourself that this time you're not going to give in—you're not going to let your temper, or your mouth, or that particularly attractive temptation run away with you. But when it comes right down to it, you don't seem to be able to control yourself. ▶ Some days it just seems easier to go with the flow than to try to put on the brakes. ▶ But guess what? Either we choose to use self-control . . . or do whatever we want and end up enslaved to our desires. ▶ So here's the question: Do you want to control your desires, or do you want them to control you? ▶ "A man is a slave to whatever has mastered him" (2 Peter 2:19).

1 It's All in Your Mind

The gym at 2:30, Friday afternoon: ▶ Enter Doug and Gene who suddenly notice about a dozen members of the school dance team going through a routine. ▶ Gene (excitedly whispering): "Would you look at Pam Powers! She's unbelievable! I sure wish . . ." [Common decency prevents us from printing the rest of his remarks—eds.] ▶ Doug looks at Pam. Then again. Then a third time. In fact, he can't get his eyes or his mind off her. And, as you might imagine, it's not because he's marveling at the talent God has given her in the art of dance.

look it up —• One of the toughest assignments Christians have is self-control of the mind. How can you make sure your thought life is pleasing to God?

- "Set your minds on things above, not on earthly things" (Colossians 3:2).

- "Finally, brothers, whatever is true, whatever is noble, whatever is right, whatever is pure, whatever is lovely, whatever is admirable—if anything is excellent or praiseworthy—think about such things" (Philippians 4:8).

Self-control of the mind doesn't just happen. We gain self-control when we deliberately choose moment by moment to fill our minds with pure, godly thoughts and not with impure, godless ones.

think it through —• The human mind is an incredible creation. It's there that we reason, think, predict, use stored information, decide, analyze, believe, and develop attitudes. And, of course, how we think determines how we live—our behavior.

No wonder God's Word is so insistent that we "renew our minds" (Romans 12:2; Ephesians 4:23).

Our ability to live for God directly depends on the way we use our minds.

work it out —• Much of what comes into our minds enters through our eyes. Doug can choose to feed lustful thoughts by ogling Pam, or he can consciously focus elsewhere. What are the visual triggers that start unhealthy thought patterns for you? What can you do to break that train of thought?

Here's a guarantee: Spend time every day reading, memorizing, and studying God's Word, and you'll have more control over your thought life.

nail it down —• Read Psalm 10:4.

Self-control

2) The Tongue—A Lethal Weapon

Friday, 3:35 P.M. in the parking lot after school: ▶ Suzanne: "Can you believe Heidi? I mean, did you see her coming on to Ross at lunch?" ▶ Christine: "I know, I can't stand her! She's such a tease." ▶ Suzanne: "What do you mean, 'tease'? She's trash! She's been with just about the whole football team." ▶ Christine (shocked): "Has she really?" ▶ Suzanne: "Oh come on, Chris! Everybody knows that! Where have you been?"

look it up —• The tongue can be a lethal weapon! So often we use it to gossip, curse, complain, criticize, lie, ridicule, or insult. But, as usual, God has some better ideas for this muscle he created:

- "Reckless words pierce like a sword, but the tongue of the wise brings healing" (Proverbs 12:18).

- "An anxious heart weighs a man down, but a kind word cheers him up" (Proverbs 12:25).

- "Do not let any unwholesome talk come out of your mouths, but only what is helpful for building others up according to their needs, that it may benefit those who listen" (Ephesians 4:29).

think it through —• Have you ever had the foolish feeling, "Why did I say that?" Have you ever

been in a heated argument, said something really cruel, and immediately thought, *Did I just say that out loud?*

As with anything in the Christian life, verbal self-control isn't something we master in a minute. It takes practice. Self-control is the result of a big decision— following Jesus in general— applied to numerous little decisions—following him in each specific situation.

work it out —• Make this your prayer today: "God, I run my mouth way too much and say a lot of things I shouldn't. I want to use my mouth to help others, not to rip them apart. Take control of my tongue. Remind me to speak only at appropriate times and only in appropriate ways."

Then go out and find a friend who's having a bad day. Tell them why you appreciate them. A genuine compliment goes a long way toward building up and benefiting someone who is listening to you.

nail it down —• Read Proverbs 21:23.

pray about it —•

Self-Control

Seeing Red

At the Macklin residence tempers are flaring. ▶ Kirk (his voice rising): "I'm not telling you again—get off the phone!" ▶ Caitlyn: "Shut up, Kirk! I'll be off in a minute." ▶ Kirk (yelling): "You just talked to her at school. Can't you live one minute without your stupid friends?" ▶ Caitlyn: "At least I *have* friends." ▶ Kirk: "Only because they feel sorry for you because Corey dumped you for Melissa!" ▶ Caitlyn (throwing a shoe at Kirk): "You pig! Get out!"

look it up —• In a world full of bully brothers and sarcastic sisters, it's easy for a minor squabble to turn into a major conflict. Solomon gives us some wisdom for controlling our tempers:

- "Better a patient man than a warrior, a man who controls his temper than one who takes a city" (Proverbs 16:32).

- "Do not make friends with a hot-tempered man, do not associate with one easily angered, or you may learn his ways and get yourself ensnared" (Proverbs 22:24–25).

- "An angry man stirs up dissension, and a hot-tempered one commits many sins" (Proverbs 29:22).

think it through —• Have you ever been an uninvolved bystander and watched someone completely lose it? By allowing their tempers to get the best of them, they ended up making fools of themselves and embarrassing everyone they were with.

Do you know someone who is quick-tempered? Are you? What situations tend to get you the angriest in the shortest amount of time?

work it out —• The next time you get in a high-voltage situation (like the one above), try calling a literal timeout. Go somewhere else for as long as it takes to get a clear head.

When you can be more objective, ask yourself, "Who's in control of my life right now—God? . . . or my temper?"

Stop. Make sure his Spirit is calling the shots.

Then go back and resolve the problem without ranting and raving, without saying and doing things you'll regret later.

nail it down —• Read Proverbs 14:17.

Self-control

4 Some Like It Hot

look it up —▸ Having self-control over your sexual desires is difficult. Not impossible by any means, but difficult. Maybe that's why God's Word has so many warnings on this subject. For example:

"Live by the Spirit, and you will not gratify the desires of the sinful nature.... The acts of the sinful nature are obvious: sexual immorality, impurity and debauchery.... But the fruit of the Spirit is ... self-control.... Those who belong to Christ Jesus have crucified the sinful nature with its passions and desires. Since we live by the Spirit, let us keep in step with the Spirit" (Galatians 5:16–25).

think it through —▸ Life is full of choices. When it comes to sexual desires, you have basically two options. You can either

1. listen to your sinful nature, "go for it" sexually, and end up a slave of your passions; or

2. live according to God's Word and experience the freedom of self-control.

Most teens who are honest about their experiences will tell you that choice #1 angers God, produces guilt and frustration, and ruins relationships. Choice #2 pleases God, produces character and respect, and strengthens relationships.

work it out —▸ The time to start developing sexual self-control is not when you find yourself in the backseat of a car in the dark corner of a parking lot. If you're serious about staying sexually pure, set yourself some boundaries now—before you get into a tempting situation. A good way to start is by listing places you know set you up for temptation (like being alone together in an otherwise empty house) and committing to stay away from those places.

If you're having trouble exercising self-control in your dating life, pray this prayer: "Lord, I've really sinned by getting too physical in my relationships, and I want to come back to what's right. Forgive me and give me your strength so that I can say no to my sinful nature. Give me the wisdom to avoid tempting situations in the future."

nail it down —▸ Read 1 Corinthians 6:9–11.

pray about it —▸

Self-Control

Couch-Potato Syndrome

A typical home at 4:40 on Saturday afternoon: ▶ Vanessa (to her brother Rich, as she walks through the family room): "Rich, you couch potato! All you do is lay there and watch TV." ▶ Rich: "So—all you do is go in the kitchen and stuff your face." ▶ Vanessa: "At least I have a life." ▶ Rich: "At least I can fit through the door." ▶ Vanessa: "Why don't you grow up?" ▶ Rich: "Why don't you shut up?"

look it up —• We've included the exchange between Rich and Vanessa because it shows two more ways we often fail at self-control: overeating and wasting time.

Regarding our tendency to overindulge in life's pleasures, Paul warned, "'Everything is permissible for me'—but not everything is beneficial. 'Everything is permissible for me'—but I will not be mastered by anything" (1 Corinthians 6:12).

Regarding time management, Paul said, "Be very careful, then, how you live—not as unwise but as wise, making the most of every opportunity, because the days are evil" (Ephesians 5:15–16).

think it through —• Many people eat when they're not hungry or keep eating when they're already full. Is the real solution a new diet, or is it exercising self-control?

Many teenagers spend several hours each day watching the tube or surfing the Web. How many spend as much time getting to know God better?

work it out —• Here are some tips on how to take control:

1. Get together with a friend who's also struggling. Agree to pray together about your problem every day for two weeks. (You'll need God's strength to succeed.)

2. Set specific goals like "I'm not eating between meals" or "I'm only watching one hour of TV each day."

3. Keep each other on track. Call your "control partner" and ask, "Is the TV off? Are you making the most of your time?"

nail it down —• Read Galatians 5:24. This weekend read an amazing story of self-control: Matthew 4:1–10.

Self-Control

topic ─────────────────────┐

Tough Questions

looking for answers?

Scary question: "Would you like to go out Friday night?" ▶ Silly question: "Did Adam and Eve have belly buttons?" ▶ Important questions (Not "Can I have the car tonight?" but life-and-death stuff. Hard questions about what's really true and what matters—all with eternal consequences):

- Is there a God?

- Who is Jesus Christ?

- Is Christ the only way to God?

- Is the Bible really true?

- How can I know for sure I'm going to heaven?

Keep reading; there are answers! ▶ "Always be prepared to give an answer to everyone who asks you to give the reason for the hope that you have" (1 Peter 3:15).

ost of the students at McKinley High like Mr. Wells, the biology teacher, because he's funny and because it's easy to get him off the subject long enough that he forgets the weekly quiz. ❯ Last Friday someone asked him about God to get him off track. ❯ "God?" he chuckled. "Well, when I was younger I believed in God. But in college, I came to believe that the universe was created by chance and that only physical things—things you can see, hear, touch, taste, and smell—exist."

look it up —• We all encounter people in life who think God doesn't exist. God, of course, disagrees.

"The fool says in his heart, 'There is no God'" (Psalm 14:1).

"Since the creation of the world God's invisible qualities—his eternal power and divine nature—have been clearly seen, being understood from what has been made" (Romans 1:20).

think it through —• There are two fatal flaws in Mr. Wells's belief. First, a chance universe doesn't account for the evidence of intelligent design all around us. The genetic information found in a single cell is like the information found in Mr. Wells's biology textbook—highly specified, highly complex.

Does Mr. Wells believe that his textbook had no intelligent designer? Not a chance. Then why does he believe chance can explain the design of the universe?

Second, a strictly physical universe doesn't account for moral laws. You don't doubt that some things are morally wrong—for example, child abuse, murder, and rape. But can you see, hear, or touch the concept *wrong*? How about the concept *right*? But if only physical things exist, there is no such thing as *right* or *wrong*.

Does Mr. Wells believe torturing infants is as moral as feeding them? Not a chance. Then why does he believe in a universe in which there can be no nonphysical moral laws?

work it out —• Look at the life all around you. Either you are meaningless—the result of a cosmic accident billions of years ago—or else a good Creator exists and designed you for his good purpose. How will you live—meaninglessly or purposefully?

nail it down —• Read Acts 17:22–31.

When the Creator Visited This Planet

2

Reid and Jay are hanging out, watching television after school. After listening to Judge Judy insult a few plaintiffs, they flip the channel and find three guys wrapped in white sheets on the Oprah Winfrey talk show. ▶ It turns out all three are gurus from India. Each one claims to be God. ▶ After watching them argue for about five minutes, Reid turns to Jay and says, "If any one of those guys really was God, the world would be in serious trouble!"

look it up —• When someone says, "I'm God," we need to check out his credentials. Do his words, character, and behavior support his claim?

Jesus said, "I tell you the truth, . . . before Abraham was born, I am!" (John 8:58). When Jesus said "I am," he was speaking the name of God that no Jew would dare utter and thus claiming to be God. That's why his adversaries "picked up stones to stone him" (v. 59).

Jesus backed up his claim.

- He demonstrated authority over the physical world: He calmed storms (Mark 4:39) and healed various sicknesses (Mark 3:10).

- He exercised authority over the spiritual realm by casting out demons (Luke 4:35).

- He displayed authority over death by raising others (John 11:43–44) as well as himself (John 2:19).

- He taught that people should worship only God (Matthew 4:10) and then accepted worship (John 20:28)!

think it through —• We can't say Christ was merely a good man, a great teacher, or an example. There are only two options: Christ was either God or a bad man.

If he was truly a good man, he was God; for good men tell the truth, and he claimed to be God. If he was not God, he was a bad man; for his claim to be God was either a lie or was an insane delusion. And most of us don't consider liars and deluded egomaniacs to be good men.

work it out —• Thank Christ for being willing to leave the perfection of heaven in order to come to a sinful world and die for you.

nail it down —• Read Hebrews 1:1–3, 8.

pray about it —•

A Narrow Way Is Better Than No Way

Claire is confused when she sees a popular advice column. ❯ It seems a woman has written in to complain that her grown children, who are committed Christians, are trying to persuade her to believe in Jesus Christ. She tells the columnist that she resents their "preaching," but at the same time she wonders if what they say is true. ❯ The columnist replies that all religions worship the same God, and he allows everyone into heaven. She concludes by telling the advice-seeker not to worry, because "there are many ways to God." ❯ Some of Claire's friends have been telling her the same thing. She's starting to wonder—is she right to say that Jesus is the only way, or is she being narrow-minded?

look it up —• A lot of people believe that there are many ways to God. Did Jesus?

- "I am the way and the truth and the life. No one comes to the Father except through me" (John 14:6).

- "I am the gate; whoever enters through me will be saved" (John 10:9).

Notice Jesus didn't say that he was only one of many ways or gates. He said, "No one comes to the Father except through me." That's totally exclusive.

When Jesus made those claims, he was either telling the truth, lying, or mistaken. Those are the only options. And considering that Jesus was God in human form, somehow the last two options don't seem very likely.

think it through —• Imagine everyone in your city is starving. But a gigantic grocery store is giving out free food to anyone who will come inside and receive it.

Would it make sense to stand outside and complain that the store only had one entrance? Can you imagine someone saying, "I want to get inside by going through the roof and they're saying I can't. How unfair can you get!"

So why do people complain about Christ being the only way to God? Better one way than no way!

work it out —• Are you counting on reaching God by being a good, sincere person? Forget it.

If you've never turned from your sins and trusted Christ alone for salvation, please do so right now!

If you've already trusted him, ask God for a chance to discuss your beliefs today. A lot of your friends are standing outside the "grocery store" of heaven, starving spiritually. Show them the entrance: Jesus Christ!

nail it down —• Memorize Acts 4:12.

Tough Questions

The Book Is Not Just Any Book

Colleen and Paula are talking to Tom, their youth pastor. He's holding a bunch of books.

▶ "What's all that?" Colleen asks.

▶ "Well, this Sunday we're going to study about how we know the Bible is really from God. These are all books considered holy by other religions."

▶ Paula is stunned. "You mean some people don't believe the Bible?" ▶ Tom smiles. "Well, the Mormons have the Book of Mormon; Muslims believe in the Koran; Hare Krishnas use a book I can't even pronounce; Christian Scientists read stuff written by Mary Baker Eddy . . ."

look it up —• With so many groups claiming to have "God's Word," it's nice to know the Bible is trustworthy.

The Old Testament is constantly punctuated by the phrases "this is the word of the LORD" and "then the LORD said."

The New Testament says "all Scripture is God-breathed" (2 Timothy 3:16).

Perhaps the authors of all those more recent books listed by Tom should consider this warning:

"Every word of God is flawless. . . . Do not add to his words, or he will rebuke you and prove you a liar" (Proverbs 30:5–6).

think it through —• Despite being written by more than 40 authors over a period of about 1,600 years, the Bible displays amazing unity and continuity.

Despite persecution, perversion, criticism, abuse, and time, the Bible has survived virtually intact.

What's more, the Bible is completely accurate with respect to history, archaeology, and prophecy.

Finally, the Bible has had a greater impact on culture, thought, and the lives of individuals than any other book.

What other book can truthfully make such claims?

work it out —• Since the Bible is really the Word of the living God, then it only makes sense that you ought to learn as much about it as you can. Read and think about the Bible daily, and memorize as much of it as you can.

Establish that habit early in life; later in life, you'll be so glad you did.

nail it down —• Read Psalm 119:105.

pray about it —•

One day while staying after school to work on their term papers, Debbie and Gil got into a conversation about church. That led to a serious discussion about Christianity (not a typical conversation in the library). ▶ "Look, I don't understand everything about it . . . I just know when I die, I'm going to heaven," Debbie finally said. ▶ Gil shook his head. "Man—I wish I could be so sure. But I'm afraid I've done too many wrong things. I *hope* I'll go to heaven—but I don't know."

look it up —• You may be surprised at how many people think like Gil. They believe that when you die, God takes all your good works and bad works and dumps them on a huge, cosmic scale. If the good outweighs the bad, you're in. If the opposite is true, well. . .

When it comes to something so important, God doesn't want us to be in the dark. He spells it right out so there's no guesswork.

"God has given us eternal life, and this life is in his Son. He who has the Son has life; he who does not have the Son of God does not have life. I write these things to you who believe in the name of the Son of God so that you may know that you have eternal life" (1 John 5:11–13).

think it through —• It boils down to this: If you "have the Son," you have eternal life and are headed for heaven. To say you "have the Son" is just another way of saying you believe in Jesus. You trust him (and him alone) to forgive your sins and make you right with God.

work it out —• Maybe for a class in sociology or history your teacher would let you conduct a survey on "Religious Beliefs of Students at _____ High School." One of the questions might be: "Assuming you believe in God and in a real place called heaven, how does one get to heaven?"

Not only would this help you find out what your friends believe, but you might also get an opportunity to share with some of them what the Bible says on the subject.

nail it down —• Read John 5:24. On Saturday read Paul's answer to some tough questions: Romans 9:19–21. On Sunday read Solomon's answer: Ecclesiastes 12:13–14.

 topic

Knowing God

who in the world is he?

Who is God? The man upstairs? A force? A tyrant? A cosmic Santa Claus? This week become a theologian (one who studies about God) and join us as we check out what God is *really* like. You might be surprised. You might even be shocked. But one thing is sure: your relationship with him will never be the same! ▶ "Let not the wise man boast of his wisdom or the strong man boast of his strength or the rich man boast of his riches, but let him who boasts boast about this: that he understands and knows me, that I am the LORD" (Jeremiah 9:23–24).

Ellen feels frustrated. All her life she's heard about God. In her Bible she's read about God. She and her Christian friends talk about God. Ellen believes in God, and seven years ago she became a child of God by trusting Christ as her Savior. But every now and then she feels like something's missing. . . . ▶ "Sometimes I wish I could actually see God. Or when I feel really down, have him reach out and give me a big hug. Wouldn't it be great to have him right there with you all the time? Wow! Then you'd never doubt again!"

look it up ––• Ever feel like Ellen? Most of us do at one time or another. It's easy to dismiss whatever can't be perceived with the senses. This attitude even affects Christians, making us doubt. The frustration comes because God can't be known on those terms.

Why? Because "God is spirit" (John 4:24).

What does that mean? It means he is, by nature, invisible. He doesn't have a material body like we do. And since he's not confined to a body in a specific location, he can be everywhere at once! He is right there with Ellen wherever she is, and at the same time he is with you and me!

think it through ––• If God doesn't have a physical body, why do some Bible verses mention his "ears" (1 Peter 3:12) or his "hands" (Psalm 19:1)? Such passages don't mean that God literally has a body. Those are figures of speech intended to show that God, though Spirit, can do those acts that require body parts in a man. The examples just given mean that God can hear our prayers and help us in our time of need.

Yes, sometimes the Bible records instances in which men "saw" God (Exodus 24:10; Genesis 18:1; Isaiah 6:1). But these individuals saw manifestations of God, not his invisible essence (John 1:18).

work it out ––• Thank God that, because he is spirit—not limited to a material body—he can be everywhere at once. Thank him for being with you right this very minute. As you go through the day, remember you are always in his presence.

The next step? Live like it!

nail it down ––• Read John 1:1–18.

2 A Big God = Small Problems

Brent is the kind of guy who's always "up." ❚ Today, however, Brent is depressed. In social studies they talked about the threat of terrorism. At church this evening he heard a visiting missionary talk about the billions of people in hundreds of countries around the world who are lost without Christ. Suddenly, Brent feels overwhelmed—very small, very insignificant, and very powerless. What can he possibly do to make a difference in such a desperate and dying world?

look it up —• Isaiah 40 can help Brent remember the greatness and power of God: "Who has measured the waters in the hollow of his hand, or with the breadth of his hand marked off the heavens?" (v. 12).

In other words, God is so big he could (if he wanted to) "palm" the universe like Michael Jordan palms a basketball!

That's not all: "Surely the nations are like a drop in a bucket; they are regarded as dust on the scales" (v. 15).

Imagine all of Canada and the United States—thousands of miles of plains, deserts, forests, lakes, rivers, mountains, and valleys. Yet God is so big that, to him, both of these nations are like tiny specks of dust or little drops of water.

Wait, there's more: "He brings princes to naught and reduces the rulers of this world to nothing" (v. 23). God, not world leaders, is ultimately in charge of his world.

think it through —• If God really is as awesome and powerful as these verses say he is, why do you think we so often get so worried about so many things? Do most Christians treat their majestic and great God as they should? Do you?

work it out —• List all the things that you feel incapable of doing or facing today. Write across the top of the list, "Glory and power belong to our God" (Revelation 19:1). Across the bottom write, "He gives strength to the weary and increases the power of the weak" (Isaiah 40:29).

We can make a difference in God's world because he gives his power to us.

nail it down —• Memorize Philippians 4:13.

pray about it —•

Change. Everybody goes through some changes, but Karen feels like she's in a whirlwind. When her family recently moved from Idaho to Alabama she had to break up with her boyfriend, leave all her friends, and kiss her hobby—snow-skiing—goodbye.

▶ Maybe you can identify with her anger: "Everything is always so new and different. Everything's always changing! I hate it! Why do we keep moving every other year? Why can't we just settle down somewhere and be normal?"

look it up —• Sometimes change is for the better, but sometimes it isn't. In a changing world, where can we find security? Consider these verses describing God:

"I the LORD do not change" (Malachi 3:6).

"The Father of the heavenly lights . . . does not change" (James 1:17).

God is the solid rock we can cling to and count on. Since he's perfect, he can't get better. Since he's perfect, he can't become anything less. His character is completely consistent day after day. The truth of his Word never goes out of style. He does not waver in his plans or purposes. He can't love you any more than he already does, and he'll never love you any less.

What security! What comfort! What a changeless truth for a changing world!

think it through —• Spend a couple of minutes thinking about the consistency of God. If God doesn't ever change, what does that say about

1. His love for you?

2. His attitude toward sin?

work it out —• Think of the most faithful, dependable person you know. Ask that person to share with you some tips on dependability. Then do at least one thing he or she suggests— today.

God will never, ever change in his nature, his Word, or his dealings with us! He is dependable and sure. Now that's good news!

nail it down —• Read Hebrews 13:8.

4 God's Wisdom

Andy: "I don't get it. You get to the age—14 or 15—where you start having strong feelings for someone and then your parents quote you the Bible and say, 'Now, son, we know you like Leslie a lot but you have to wait till you're married to have a sexual relationship. God's plan is that sex is only for marriage.' ▶ "Hey, I won't get married for another 10 years! That's ridiculous! God doesn't really expect that, does he?"

look it up ⟶ The real issue here isn't sex—it's God's wisdom. Wisdom is the unusual ability to understand situations and people and how to deal with them. Does God have such understanding?

"To God belong wisdom and power; counsel and understanding are his" (Job 12:13).

"He made the earth by his power; he founded the world by his wisdom and stretched out the heavens by his understanding" (Jeremiah 51:15).

Hundreds of verses repeat this truth: God created the universe; therefore, he knows what he's talking about.

think it through ⟶ Every new DVD player comes with an owner's manual. This booklet describes how the player is put together, how to hook it up, how to use it, and what to do if you have problems. Most people don't read their manual. They bury it in some drawer and then wonder six months later why they can never get to the special features on their DVDs.

We sometimes do the same thing with God. Having made us, he knows what's best for us and how we can have the most satisfying life possible. He's provided an "owner's manual" for us—the Bible—so that we can maximize our performance for him. But if we ignore his wisdom, we can end up like a disconnected DVD player.

work it out ⟶ In what areas of your life do you need God's wisdom right now? Jot them down, then talk to God about them, one at a time, claiming his promise to share his wisdom with his children (Ephesians 1:17).

nail it down ⟶ Read James 1:5.

pray about it ⟶

One thing really bothers P.J. ❱ "I know God is all powerful—just look at all the miracles in the Old Testament, or the stars and oceans. And I know he is wise; he knows what's best. ❱ "But . . . well, I guess I'm just afraid God isn't always good. I mean, if God is really as good as people say he is, why does he allow so many incredibly horrible things to happen in the world?"

look it up —• According to the Bible, the issue of God's goodness is settled: God is good!

"The LORD is good to all; he has compassion on all he has made" (Psalm 145:9).

How does God show his goodness? "The LORD upholds all those who fall and lifts up all who are bowed down" (v. 14). He opens his hand and satisfies "the desires of every living thing" (v. 16). He is "loving toward all he has made" (v. 17). He is "near to all who call on him" (v. 18). And He "watches over all who love him" (v. 20).

think it through —• Why then is there evil in the world? Because Adam chose—and people choose—to sin.

Why did God allow Adam to do such a bad thing? Though the answer is ultimately a mystery, some have answered that God was good in creating Adam with free choice—the ability to sin or not to sin. To God, apparently, creating Adam free, but able to sin, was a higher good than creating Adam sinless, but unable to be free.

Think of all the people who drown every year. Suppose we passed laws that no one could swim, ski, surf, fish, sail, or go anywhere near any body of water. With such laws we could eliminate most drownings. But the freedom to enjoy the water is a higher good than eliminating all water accidents.

work it out —• Jot down all the ways God has shown his goodness to you. Include spiritual as well as material blessings. Try to list at least 25 good things. (And then spend some time thanking him!)

nail it down —• Memorize Psalm 106:1. On Saturday, read about the ultimate act of goodness: Romans 5:8. On Sunday, memorize that verse too.

Many Ways to God

People committed to affirming the validity of all beliefs and practices would have us believe that we can get in touch with God and become whole individuals through any of the following techniques:

Yoga, transcendental meditation, transchanneling, holistic medicine, rebirthing, REIKI, psychic art, astrology, hypnotherapy, astral projection, past-life therapy, metaphysics, dream analysis, handwriting analysis, floating in isolation tanks, iridology, reflexology, body electronics, positive self-imaging, internal visualization, numerology, past-life regression, psychic readings, Shustah cards, contacting UFOs and extraterrestrials, relaxation techniques, chanting, sandplay therapy, self-hypnosis, EST and/or Forum, biofeedback, levitation, parapsychology, Silva mind control, Tarot card readings, Rolfing, martial arts, bioenergetics, crystals, positive self-talk, and T'ai Chi (provided, of course, that you have the bucks to get involved in these often extremely expensive practices!).

Compare all this with what Jesus Christ said:

"I am the way and the truth and the life. No one comes to the Father except through me" (John 14:6).

A simple statement. An exclusive statement. Jesus didn't say he was *a* way, but *the* way. That means relying on other religions is, at best, an expensive mistake; at worst, a horrible pack of lies.

If you haven't trusted Christ yet, do so right now. Tell him that you want to be forgiven of your sins, that you want to know God, and that you want to experience the true life that only he can bring. (And don't forget to thank him that his gift of eternal life is free!)

Life in Bible Times

A Long School Year, But What a Recess!"

In New Testament times, only boys received a formal education outside the home. For them, school was a year-round proposition. However, during the hot summer months, classes were limited to about four hours per day with a midday break from ten in the morning until three in the afternoon!

"A Quality Alternative to TV."

It was typical for the men in the Jewish village to gather daily after the evening meal. Sitting in a large circle, the men would relate the events of the day or tell stories from ages past. Together they would sing, laugh, and swap proverbs. Older boys would stand on the edge of the circle and listen attentively.

"Please Keep Your Knees Off the Table!"

In ancient Palestine, "tables" were actually circular pieces of skin or leather that were laid on the floor. These "tables" had loops around their edges and a drawstring through the loops. After each meal, the skin was brushed off, the cord was tightened, and the "table" was hung on the wall.

"You Ate What?"

Rich Roman feasts (perhaps like the one mentioned in Matthew 14:6–12) included exotic appetizers like jellyfish and fungi. The main course would then feature an exquisite delicacy like flamingo tongue, wild boar, or lobster with truffles. Dessert? Pastry and fruit.

"No Wonder I Feel So Tired!"

Most people slept on a rug or straw mat on the bare earthen floor. For covering they used the cloak they had worn in the day. Mattresses and pajamas were luxuries that only the wealthy and royalty enjoyed.

"Now That's What I Call a Wedding!"

A Jewish wedding ceremony was a festive procession in which a bridegroom would go to the home of his bride and bring her back to his home. There followed a party/feast that sometimes lasted more than a week.

 topic

Spiritual Warfare

boot camp for believers

S pir•it•u•al (spir'i-choo-wal, -chool), adj. 1. of the spirit or soul; not material 2. of or possessing the nature of spirit; incorporeal ▶ war•fare (wor'fer), n. 1. hostilities; war; armed conflict 2. any kind of conflict

Spiritual warfare. You can't see it or hear it. But that doesn't mean it's not real. And that doesn't mean it won't affect you. ▶ Are you ready for the battle with the Enemy? ▶ If you aren't, you need to be; the Enemy is ready for you. ▶ "Endure hardship with us like a good soldier of Christ Jesus" (2 Timothy 2:3).

There's a War Going On

What in the world is going on? ▶ Item: Large numbers of Christian marriages are ending in divorce. ▶ Item: Television preachers and local ministers are being caught in immorality. ▶ Item: 37 percent of teens say their parents don't know that they are sexually active. ▶ Item: In general people are more spiritual now but fewer of them are turning to Christianity. Instead they are seeking other religious beliefs, or forming their own.

look it up —• From Genesis to Revelation, the Bible is clear: It's war out there! This ancient spiritual struggle is just as real as the physical conflicts that take place between nations. The apostle Paul wrote:

"Finally, be strong in the Lord and in his mighty power. Put on the full armor of God so that you can take your stand against the devil's schemes. For our struggle is not against flesh and blood, but against the rulers, against the authorities, against the powers of this dark world and against the spiritual forces of evil in the heavenly realms" (Ephesians 6:10–12).

think it through —• Most people and many Christians go through life unaware of the great conflict that's raging all around

them. While they worry over trivial matters ("Did you see *Late Night* last night?" or "Do you like this outfit better or this one?"), there's a worldwide war going on—with life-and-death consequences!

What would be the chance of survival for a deaf and blind person who stumbled across a raging battlefield, not even realizing a war was in progress?

work it out —• This week is sort of like a boot camp for believers. The purpose is to make you more aware of the battle lines, and to show you how you can not only survive but also succeed. Here's a prayer for the week:

"Lord, sometimes I get so caught up in activities that I forget there's an invisible war going on all around me. Help me this week to see that the conflict is real. Both sides are playing for keeps! Show me how to stand and fight the good fight of faith. I want to be victorious for Christ, who won the victory at the cross. Amen."

nail it down —• Catch a glimpse of God's invisible armies—2 Kings 6:8–17.

2 How Well Do You Know the Enemy?

look it up —• Satan is not a product of some Hollywood special effects wizard. He's a dangerous killer.

- He is an angel who was expelled from heaven because of his rebellion against God's authority (Isaiah 14:12–15).

- He wants to destroy you. "Your enemy the devil prowls around like a roaring lion looking for someone to devour" (1 Peter 5:8).

- He met more than his match in the person of Jesus Christ: "Since the children have flesh and blood, he too shared in their humanity so that by his death he might destroy him who holds the power of death—that is, the devil—and free those who all their lives were held in slavery by their fear of death" (Hebrews 2:14–15).

think it through —• We don't want to become obsessed with Satan, or be frightened by the verses that discuss his power. We learn about him only so we can be better equipped to stand against him until Christ returns.

work it out —• If you've been dabbling in anything having to do with the occult—seances, tarot cards, crystals, astrology, Ouija boards, palm reading—stop immediately! Such practices are strictly forbidden in the Bible (see Deuteronomy 18:10–13).

But the Devil doesn't restrict himself to the obvious occult. Some of his favorite arenas for distributing his deadly ideas are politics, education, and the media.

Pay careful attention to the information you hear at school, in the news, and in entertainment media. Reject any beliefs that don't line up with the Bible. Don't give the Devil a foothold in your life.

nail it down —• Read 1 John 4:4.

pray about it —•

Combat Ready?

Wasn't that missionary speaker awesome?" Katie said to Rhonda after Sunday school. ❯ "Yeah—especially when he talked about exorcising that demon-possessed man." ❯ "That was spooky!" Katie shivered. "I'm sure glad we don't live where there are evil forces at work!" ❯ "Me too! So," Rhonda said, changing the subject, "do you want to go to the mall or the movies this afternoon?"

look it up —• According to the Bible, Christians are soldiers in God's army—whether they like it or not. The question is, What kind of soldiers are we?

Are we concentrating on his cause? We need to be. "Endure hardship with us like a good soldier of Christ Jesus. No one serving as a soldier gets involved in civilian affairs—he wants to please his commanding officer" (2 Timothy 2:3–4).

Are we prepared for battle and keeping a sharp lookout for the enemy? That should be our mindset.

"Be self-controlled and alert" (1 Peter 5:8).

think it through —• Good soldiers take advantage of their training. They obey orders and are concerned with only one thing: defeating the enemy.

Bad soldiers prefer the safety of the base. They follow orders only when they feel like it.

Which kind of soldier are you?

work it out —• Take these steps to become a good soldier:

- Consider worship, youth group, and Bible study as training. Pay close attention. Take notes. Some of the information may one day save your life!

- Obey the orders of your Commander-in-Chief. These are found in his Word, the Bible.

- Make choices not on the basis of what is easiest but on the basis of what is best. Good soldiers undertake any mission to ensure victory.

- When an activity begins to divert your focus from the Lord and his work, reevaluate your priorities.

Remember, military people can't afford to get caught up in nonmilitary business!

nail it down —• Read Ephesians 6:18.

Spiritual Warfare

4 Bracing for the Battle

he next week, Katie's youth pastor followed up on the missionary's talk by challenging students to get armed for spiritual warfare right where they live. Katie made a commitment to start making a difference for God at school. Here's what happened: ❱ When she told a friend in P.E. class about her decision, the friend responded, "Katie, quit being so righteous! Don't you think I saw you at that party last weekend?" ❱ When she took an English exam, several kids were cheating. Katie felt an incredible temptation to join in. She did, and then the guilt really piled up.

look it up —• Katie needs to know that God doesn't send his soldiers into battle unprotected.

"Put on the full armor of God, so that when the day of evil comes, you may be able to stand your ground, . . . Stand firm then, with the belt of truth buckled around your waist, with the breastplate of righteousness in place, and with your feet fitted with the readiness that comes from the gospel of peace. In addition to all this, take up the shield of faith, with which you can extinguish all the flaming arrows of the evil one. Take the helmet of salvation and the sword of the Spirit, which is the word of God" (Ephesians 6:13–17).

think it through —• What good are weapons to a soldier if he leaves all this equipment in his tent when he goes out to fight? Are you using the divine weapons God has provided (2 Corinthians 10:3–5)?

work it out —• Put on God's armor today and everyday.

- "The belt of truth"—Be a person of integrity and faithfulness. Honor your commitments.
- "The breastplate of righteousness"—Live a righteous life. It's a great protection (James 4:7).
- "Feet fitted with . . . the gospel of peace"—Be willing to take the gospel to the world.
- "The shield of faith"—Trust in the promises of God for security against the accusations and attacks of Satan.
- "The helmet of salvation"—The promise of salvation provides further confidence in battle.
- "The sword of the Spirit, which is the word of God"—This, the only offensive weapon, causes the Enemy to flee (Matthew 4:1–11). Hang on to it and use it to God's glory!

nail it down —• Read 1 Thessalonians 5:8.

pray about it —•

5 The Outcome Is Never in Doubt

espite a few setbacks (remember yesterday?), Katie stuck with her new commitment to Christ. She and Rhonda began meeting every morning to pray for each other. They agreed to read through the New Testament and to check up on each other every day. ❱ Slowly but surely these two very normal girls are becoming battle-hardened soldiers for the Lord. ❱ Through their witness they've each led a friend to the Savior! What's more, they're experiencing victory over the temptations that weeks before nailed them every time.

look it up —• Winning day-to-day battles is exciting. But even more exciting is the news that this fighting won't last forever! In our war against the forces of evil, God promises both protection and ultimate victory.

- "The Lord will rescue me from every evil attack and will bring me safely to his heavenly kingdom" (2 Timothy 4:18).

- "God is just: He will pay back trouble to those who trouble you and give relief to you who are troubled, and to us as well. This will happen when the Lord Jesus is revealed from heaven in blazing fire with his powerful angels" (2 Thessalonians 1:6–7).

think it through —• Even after the U.S. defeated Japan in World War II, many Japanese soldiers continued fighting on some of the islands in the Pacific. It took years to subdue some of these desperate men and finally end the conflict.

In the same way, Christ won the war against Satan at the Cross. The forces of evil were dealt the death blow when the Savior cried, "It is finished!" Now we're involved in the mop-up operation.

work it out —• Spend some time thanking God that he has defeated the Enemy through the blood of his Son.

Meanwhile, find a friend and do what Rhonda and Katie are doing. Begin claiming the results of Christ's victory. Pray daily for each other and for friends who don't yet know the Lord. Think of creative ways to fight Christ's battles in your area of interest.

P.S. Don't forget to put on your armor!

nail it down —• Read Romans 16:20. On Saturday, read Isaiah 53:11–12. On Sunday, read Isaiah 54:1–3 and Galatians 4:26–27 for the victorious results of the Cross.

Spiritual Warfare

topic ————————————————

Dating

winning at the dating game

O n the list of things that can make you feel like a winner or a loser in high school, dating has to be near the top. If your love life is going great, you feel like you're on top of the world. But when you "lose" at dating, it can hurt deeply and for a long time. ▶ Regardless of whether you see yourself as a winner or a loser in the "game" of dating, set aside some time this week to take a look at some of God's guidelines for dating. ▶ "Delight yourself in the LORD and he will give you the desires of your heart" (Psalm 37:4).

The Great Date Wait

Amy is in shock. She is listening to Sheila turn down Ron Summers, the hottest guy at Lincoln High, for a weekend date! ▶ "Are you brain-dead?" Amy asks when Sheila hangs up the phone. "He looks exactly like Brad Pitt! Sheila, how could you?" ▶ "I don't know. I just didn't feel right about it. I'm not sure he's a Christian." ▶ "Sheila, life just isn't fair. I hardly ever get called. And here you are turning down Ron Summers! So what if he's not a Christian? He's not asking you to marry him!"

look it up —• Amy's waiting for a call from anybody. Sheila's waiting for the right guy—a Christian guy. Who's right?

Consider these verses:

"Do not be yoked together with unbelievers.... What does a believer have in common with an unbeliever?" (2 Corinthians 6:14–15).

The phrase "yoked together" refers to the farming practice of hooking two animals side by side for the purpose of working together—perhaps pulling a plow. This passage tells us that Christians must not be paired with non-Christians in an intimate way.

think it through —• In principle, a Christian's highest goal is to live according to the standards of truth and morality taught in the Bible (John 14:15). A non-Christian's highest goal is to live according to his or her own standards of truth and morality (Romans 3:10–18).

And so, for a Christian to seriously date a non-Christian is like yoking a mule and an ox together and then trying to plow a field. The two animals want to go in different directions and at different speeds.

Sheila knows that accepting one date doesn't mean she's necessarily "yoked" to Ron. But she also knows she could easily develop feelings for Ron. She's not willing to risk falling in love with a guy who doesn't share her beliefs, in love with someone who might tempt her to lower her standards.

work it out —• On a piece of paper, list some of the potential complications and heartaches of dating a non-Christian. How many of them could you avoid if you resolve to date only committed Christians? Of course, you may (no, should) be friends with non-Christians. But beware of anything more serious than friendship!

nail it down —• Read Ephesians 5:1–8.

Dating

2   Know "Why" Before "Who"

heila and Amy are talking about the same things most teenage girls talk about: love, sex, dating, and guys at school—not necessarily in that order. Let's listen in. ❱ "Oh, Amy, at youth group last night we saw the best video on dating. Mainly it talked about what the Bible says . . . you know, the kind of people we should date and reasons for going out." ❱ "Reasons? Do I need 'reasons'? I go out because that's what everyone does—to have fun, to keep from sitting home on weekends, to find a boyfriend. Aren't those reasons good enough?"

look it up —• Amy asks a great question. What are good reasons for Christians to date? Try these:

1. To bring glory to God (1 Corinthians 10:31).

2. To encourage another Christian to grow: "And let us consider how we may spur one another on toward love and good deeds" (Hebrews 10:24).

3. To grow personally (Proverbs 27:17).

4. To prepare for marriage. As we date, we discover what kind of person would be best suited for us as a mate and how to relate well to the opposite sex.

think it through —• Many students date for all the wrong reasons. Some date for sex and end up guilt ridden and under God's curse. Some date to be in a serious relationship and end up frustrated. Some date solely to have fun or to be seen with the right people or to keep from being bored—all reasons that won't bring satisfaction.

How would your dating life change if you adopted as your top priority to bring glory to God? If you were to take a sincere interest in others, being sensitive and encouraging to them while on dates, do you think you'd have a harder or easier time getting future dates?

work it out —• Write out a list of reasons why people date. Be honest. Which of these dating goals might bring disappointment?

Now talk through this list with God. Ask him if these are reasons you should be dating. Ask him to direct you toward the way he wants you to date (or not).

nail it down —• Read Psalm 84:11.

pray about it —•

Ryan and Kevin have it planned. They're going to double-date Saturday night—eat first and then go to a movie. All they need are dates! ❯ Ryan thumbs through the school yearbook. "Look, I'll call Carol if you'll call Karen." ❯ "I don't know," Kevin replies. ❯ "Kevin," Ryan says, pointing to the yearbook, "we're talking two of the hottest girls in school." ❯ "I know. They're incredible looking! But that's not all that counts. Look, I'm tired of asking girls out just for the sake of going out. I want somebody really special."

look it up —• Maybe you can relate to Kevin's feelings. As you get older and grow as a Christian, you realize you want more in a date than someone with good looks, popularity, or lots of money.

What should a Christian look for in a potential date? Someone who takes seriously these words of Jesus: "Love the Lord your God with all your heart and with all your soul and with all your mind. . . . Love your neighbor as yourself" (Matthew 22:37–39).

In other words, the ideal person to date is someone

* who has a heart for God, someone who loves the Lord and is committed to walking with him;

* who has a heart for people, someone who's unselfish and genuinely cares about others.

think it through —• "But," you may argue, "if I only date serious Christians, I'll never have fun!" Wrong! Committed Christians can have more fun dating than anyone else!

Here's why: Knowing the rules and sticking to them frees both people to have an honest, genuine relationship with no emotional games. They can be themselves and enjoy each other.

work it out —• Think back on the last three or four people you've dated (or wanted to date). Are they really the kind of people God would have you date?

What about you? Are you living in a way that would be attractive to another committed Christian? What specific changes could you make that might make you more popular with the right kind of people?

nail it down —• Read 2 Timothy 2:22.

P.S. Kevin finally called Sheila for the big weekend.

And Ryan got a date with Sheila's friend Amy.

4 Creative Dating

evin and Ryan are stumped. They've got dates with Sheila and Amy for Saturday night, but their plan to go eat and see a movie is ruined. ❿ Both girls have already seen the only decent movie playing in town! And they have to be at the school auditorium by 5 P.M. for a Latin Club banquet! ❿ "Amy said we can pick them up at 7:00," Ryan sighs, "but they won't be hungry and they've already seen the movie. What are we going to do?"

look it up —• Christians don't have to keep doing the same old things over and over again on dates. Why? For this reason: "God created man in his own image" (Genesis 1:27).

Because we are made in God's image, we have the God-given ability to be creative. We can come up with different ideas. We can try new things. We can be unique. And believe it or not, this is true for everyone.

think it through —• Let's play "create-a-date." Think of unique things you could do on a date that would please God, enable you to get to know your date, and provide hours of fun.

Here's just a partial list: jog, play tennis, play ping-pong, swim, play basketball, cook, visit a nursing home, wash your car, ride bikes, visit people in the hospital, go to a historical site, visit a museum, take a walk, look at stars, take pictures, make your own movie, watch people at the airport, pray together, do a Bible study, have a barbecue, paint, write poetry or songs or letters, ski, volunteer to do charitable work together, go witnessing, go to a public lecture, play board games, build something, feed ducks, learn a new skill, go to the zoo, go to the library, or read to each other.

work it out —• On a scale of 1–10 (1 being boring and 10 exciting), rate your last five dating activities. Are you using the creative ability God has given you?

Think of 10 creative dates you could do for under $10. Now, don't just sit there. Get to work on your creative date plans!

nail it down —• Reflect on God's creativity in Psalm 145:11–12.

pray about it —•

5 Romance Is a Risky Business!

It's 11 P.M. on Saturday night and Kevin and Sheila and Ryan and Amy are having a great time! The guys got creative and went to Kevin's for a cake-baking contest. The girls died laughing as they watched the guys stumble all over the kitchen.

Now Ryan and Kevin are in the bathroom getting flour out of their hair. Ryan is so pumped he's about to explode: "Man, Amy is the greatest! Did you see how she keeps smiling at me? Kevin, no kidding, this is love at first sight—well, at least at first 'date'! Maybe I'll give her my senior ring next week!"

look it up —• Almost nothing can compare to the feeling of going out with someone and having everything click. But what about dating someone seriously and exclusively? Here are some biblical responses to those who date only

- for security—Only in God is there true security (Psalm 91:1–2);

- for increased sexual involvement—"Flee from sexual immorality" (1 Corinthians 6:18);

- because of infatuation—Sometimes our feelings can trick us into thinking we're in love when we're really not: "The heart is deceitful above all

things and beyond cure" (Jeremiah 17:9).

think it through —• Here are other things to consider:

- Are you old enough? (It takes real maturity to correctly handle a steady relationship.)

- Do your parents approve? (Their support makes all the difference.)

- Whom are you considering? (A solid Christian for a boyfriend or girlfriend can help you grow. But someone who's not excited about the Lord can hurt your walk.)

- Is God glorified by your relationship? (If it's not his will, it's certain to fail.)

work it out —• Evaluate your relationship based on the biblical principles we've noted. Are your motives for going steady really good ones?

Write out what you think a really good, Christ-centered dating relationship would be like. Resolve to have only that kind of relationship.

nail it down —• Read 1 Thessalonians 4:1. On Saturday, read 1 Timothy 3:1–4, a description of a godly man. On Sunday, read 1 Peter 3:1–6 about a godly woman.

Dating

You're ~~Hot Stuff~~

The night was crisp and crystal clear. I was driving to Los Angeles from Palm Springs about 11 P.M. The temperature was cool.

About 20 miles outside of Palm Springs, the city lights were gone and there wasn't another car in sight. It was just me, the hum of my Toyota, and the passion and power of Beethoven's *Symphony No. 1*.

Then I noticed the sky. The night canopy was filled with a million stars, all shining points of beautiful light. I gasped and began slowing down. I had to get out and take a look.

Having pulled off a safe distance from the highway, I turned the car off and got out. Then I looked around to make sure nobody was watching. Comfortably sure I was alone, I got on my knees, raised my hands, and sang as loud as I could: "Praise God from whom all blessings flow! . . ."

You Are More Glorious Than Nature. Most people don't react to nature's glory by shouting the Doxology. But all of us have been awestruck at a star-filled sky, a smoky gorge or valley, a rainbow-colored sunset, a glimpse of the Northern Lights.

Yes, nature is glorious. But did you know that you are much more glorious than the most awesome natural event?

What Makes Something Significant? About the expanse of the universe, the Bible says, "God set [the sun, moon, and stars] in the expanse of the sky to give light to the earth" (Genesis 1:16–17). From God's perspective, then, the earth is more significant than the stars, even though the earth is smaller. Likewise, people are more significant than the earth, even though they are smaller. "Let us make man in our image, in our likeness, and let them rule over . . . all the earth" (v. 26).

You're Hot Stuff! Do you see what that means? You, a single person, are more valuable than the whole expanse of the universe. Being made in God's own image, you have (1) a more valuable essence; and (2) a more important calling than the rest of God's creation.

The Bottom Line. Nature is God's; therefore, it must be treated with respect. Man rules nature; therefore, animals and the rest of the environment exist for us to use, enjoy, and develop. Our view of ourselves, the animal kingdom, and the rest of the environment should take these truths into account.

Hey! I guess that means that the next time I see you, I should extend my arms toward you and sing, "Praise God from whom all blessings flow! . . ."

That's this editor's viewpoint. Maybe you could see it that way too.

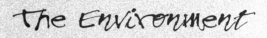

The Environment

"Paper or plastic?" the bagboy at the grocery store asks. In your mind you think, "Who cares?"

And yet, your choice will affect the world around you. Answer paper and you indirectly vote to chop down another tree. Answer plastic and, in a roundabout way, you help drill another oil well since plastic is a petroleum product.

Small Decisions—Big Consequences. Other choices are important as well. Driving a car instead of riding the bus contributes to the "greenhouse effect," a global warming trend caused by excessive carbon dioxide in the air. Buying aerosol hair spray or Styrofoam plates means releasing chloroflourocarbons that destroy the earth's protective ozone shield. Washing clothes with detergents that contain phosphates means altering the delicate balance of life in streams, lakes, and rivers.

Multiply these "little" choices by the millions of people living in overcrowded industrialized societies, throw in other pressing problems such as what to do about acid rain and nuclear waste, and it's no wonder environmentalists are concerned.

The Bible and the Environment. The Bible states that after God created the heavens and the earth (Genesis 1:1), He created man and woman. Then the Creator gave his human creatures authority to "subdue" the earth (Genesis 1:28).

Some people use this command as a license for exploitation. The earth's resources are depleted in order to support extravagant and greedy lifestyles. No thought is given to the facts that these resources are limited and non-renewable or that their careless consumption contributes to the world's pollution problems.

Others see Genesis 1:28 as a call to conservation. The human race is to act as a caretaker of creation. The goal is not to conquer the environment. We are to conserve it for future use and pleasure (see Genesis 2:15).

What Now? Because of the condition of our planet, Christians must be more concerned about the environment. And our concern must lead to action. Ecological preservation and protection, not pollution, should mark those who follow Christ.

 **topic**

Myths

exposing false notions

A myth is like a birthday package without a gift. Though it's nicely wrapped on the outside, it turns out to be empty on the inside. ▶ If you think myths ended with ancient Rome, I'd like you to meet the Brightsides, a nice Christian family. Each Brightside believes a different modern myth. ▶ Let's spend a week with this family. Who knows? You might discover that you believe some empty myths too! ▶ "The discerning heart seeks knowledge, but the mouth of a fool feeds on folly" (Proverbs 15:14).

Trusting in Material Wealth

Bill Brightside makes a few calls on his earphone as he waits in traffic. "Time is money, right?" he asks rhetorically as he wheels and deals with clients. We finally arrive at his corporate headquarters. He leads the way into a spacious and very elegant office. We sit down. ❯ "My business philosophy is simple," he begins. "I grew up poor and I know that without money, you just can't do much in this world, right? ❯ "Now, I admit, my 14-hour days keep me away from the family and church. But I like to think of all this as making money for God."

look it up —• Is Mr. Brightside making money for God? Or is he making money his god? A lot of people buy into the idea that money means happiness. But it's not necessarily so.

Jesus told the story of a foolish rich man who said to himself, "'You have plenty of good things laid up for many years. Take life easy; eat, drink and be merry.'

"But God said to him, 'You fool! This very night your life will be demanded from you. Then who will get what you have prepared for yourself?'

"This is how it will be with anyone who stores up things for him-self but is not rich toward God" (Luke 12:19–21).

think it through —• Money can be stolen, jewelry can be lost, property can be seized or destroyed. There's never a time when any of it is guaranteed 100 percent safe! The view that money is ultimately trustworthy is a modern myth.

Do you know Christians like Mr. Brightside? Are you like him?

work it out —• If you answered yes to that last question, do two things:

• Pray. "Father, I have an idol. I trust more in material things than I do in you. I know that's wrong. Please change me. Show me ways to decrease my dependence on things. Cause my trust in you to increase— by the power of Christ. Amen."

• Reflect on 1 Timothy 6:17–19 every day this week.

Then, if you have extra material possessions or wealth, willingly use some to help someone less fortunate. (See Acts 4:32–35.)

nail it down —• Read Proverbs 11:28.

Myths

2) Thinking That Sin Brings Fulfillment

Bonnie Brightside, 17, is feeling pretty grown-up and very ready to get out from under the thumb of her overprotective mother. She wants to hurry up and get to college and experience life on her own. ▶ Sitting in her bedroom, Bonnie opens up. "All Mom lets me do is go to church. I miss out on all the fun in life! I'm dying to know what it's like to be the life of the party . . . to get high and really loosen up . . . to make love to a handsome stranger. Well, my life may be boring right now, but when I get to college I'm really going to make up for lost time."

look it up —• Bonnie is on the verge of making some big mistakes. She believes the myth that sin satisfies. But that's been the Devil's lie since the beginning of time.

"'You will not surely die,' the serpent said to the woman. 'For God knows that when you eat of it your eyes will be opened, and you will be like God, knowing good and evil.'

"When the woman saw that the fruit of the tree was good for food and pleasing to the eye, and also desirable for gaining wisdom, she took some and ate it. She also gave some to her husband" (Genesis 3:4–6).

The result? Sorrow, tragedy, death. In a word, sin brought dissatisfaction, both divine and human.

think it through —• The rich, exotic dishes look too good to pass up. So you eat. The food tastes too good to believe. But then you realize the chef is really a deranged murderer. You've been poisoned!

Satan does that. He always makes sin look appealing and enticing. But those who eat end up burned.

work it out —• Here are 3 Rs for avoiding this world's favorite myth—the idea that sin satisfies:

• Renew your mind. Change your way of thinking! Cut out the worldly input—the movies, TV, magazines, songs—that make light of sin and warp your values.

• Recognize temptations when they come. Be on your guard. Otherwise, you could be fooled by some innocent-looking bait.

• Reject the offer to sin. Think about the consequences, especially about displeasing the Lord, who loved you enough to die for you.

nail it down —• Read Hebrews 11:24–28.

pray about it —•

Myths

3 Overemphasizing External Things

Mrs. Betty Brightside is a very pretty woman who attends a daily aerobics class faithfully. Always well-dressed, she makes sure that her home is spotless. She's proud of her public image and of the status she and her husband have in the community. ▶ "I think people ought to be able to look at us Christians and see a difference," she says. "For example, take that Jo Ellen Nash who works at the church. She's the sweetest thing, helping the homeless and all. But the poor thing needs to lose at least 75 pounds! Her appearance is just awful!"

look it up —• Mrs. Brightside is right. Christians should be different. However, the difference must be more than merely external. Jesus said people can look great on the outside and still be rotten on the inside.

"'Woe to you, teachers of the law and Pharisees, you hypocrites! You are like whitewashed tombs, which look beautiful on the outside but on the inside are full of dead men's bones and everything unclean'" (Matthew 23:27).

He also said, "Stop judging by mere appearances, and make a right judgment" (John 7:24).

think it through —• Is it wrong to look nice or try to get in shape or to have nice clothes? No! But it is wrong to have a "Betty Brightside" perspective on life and judge everyone and everything by outer appearance.

Did the ragtag band of disciples who followed Jesus have a good public image? Not if "good public image" means they possessed the symbols of success.

How do you think God views success and spirituality? Can a person have only one or the other? Can a person have both?

work it out —• Say no to the myth that external appearance is more important than internal health. Here's how:

- Don't isolate the spiritual from the physical. View all the events of life—personal grooming, exercise, school, work, prayer, Bible reading— as God's gifts to you for the advancement of his kingdom.

- Quit judging other people on the basis of appearance. Don't write people off just because they are short, overweight, handicapped, poor, or different from you in some other way.

nail it down —• Read 2 Corinthians 10:7.

Myths

4 Trusting Only in Yourself

Nice-looking, smart, athletic, popular—that's Biff Brightside. ❱ People are always telling him how talented he is. And it's true. He doesn't really have to work to make good grades, friends, or touchdowns. ❱ Biff thinks he's got the world by the tail. ❱ "I feel really confident in my abilities. If I put my mind to something, I know I can do it. Things have always come pretty easy for me so far, but even if I get in a tough situation, I don't have any doubt that I can handle it. I know I can come out on top through hard work."

look it up —• What many people consider the admirable quality of confidence is often nothing more than cockiness—trusting only in one's own abilities. To such an attitude, God's Word says:

- "Cursed is the one who trusts in man, who depends on flesh for his strength and whose heart turns away from the LORD" (Jeremiah 17:5).

- "He who trusts in himself is a fool, but he who walks in wisdom is kept safe" (Proverbs 28:26).

- "So, if you think you are standing firm, be careful that you don't fall!" (1 Corinthians 10:12).

Sheesh. So much for self-sufficiency.

think it through —• Do you count on solely your own ability to ace that English exam, make that free throw, land a date for the weekend, talk to someone about the Lord, put together a project, impress your employer, make new friends, or talk in front of a group? If so, you've got a pride problem.

work it out —• Here are some tips for abandoning the myth of self-sufficiency:

1. *Confess.* Thoughts like "I can do this on my own" or "Look at what I've done without any help from anyone!" are offensive to God (Daniel 4:30–32).

2. *Submit.* Jesus Christ is Lord. *Lord* means "master." Because of who he is, you must do what he wants and depend ultimately on his strength (Psalm 28:7).

3. *Pray.* Ask God to sanctify every activity in which you're involved (1 Thessalonians 5:17). It's hard to trust in yourself while you're talking to God.

nail it down —• Read Isaiah 2:22.

pray about it —•

Myths

5 Presuming on the Future

ob Brightside is Bonnie's twin brother. He's also eager to get that high school diploma because he's already got his whole life planned out. ❭ "I'm going to go to the University of Virginia and study finance and international relations. Then I'm going to get a law degree and start my own import-exporting firm with offices all over the world." ❭ What about church responsibilities and a close walk with Christ? ❭ "I'll worry about all that when I'm older, married, and ready to settle down and have a family."

look it up —• One of the great modern myths is assuming that we have the right and ability to dictate our own future. James offers a different perspective:

"Now listen, you who say, 'Today or tomorrow we will go to this or that city, spend a year there, carry on business and make money.' Why, you do not even know what will happen tomorrow. What is your life? You are a mist that appears for a little while and then vanishes. Instead, you ought to say, 'If it is the Lord's will, we will live and do this or that.' As it is you boast and brag. All such boasting is evil" (James 4:13–16).

think it through —• Is it wrong to make plans for the future? Is it wrong to live as though we alone are the masters of our destiny? Remember, God is the Lord of history; nobody escapes from his gaze; and no plans we make fool him or overrule him.

work it out —• Don't plan your life independently. Plan your world in light of God's Word. For example, here are some pointers in planning a career:

1. Look at the way God has made you. What are you good at? What do you enjoy? What are your strengths? Your weaknesses?

2. Look for a career that fits the way God made you. Is there a field that interests you? Given your strengths, would you be good at it?

3. Pray. Ask God to move in your life to confirm or deny the direction you want to go. And ask him to prevent you from making anything—including a career—an idol.

nail it down —• Read Proverbs 19:21. On Saturday, read Proverbs 16:9. On Sunday, read Proverbs 16:3 for a real encouragement.

Myths

God's Will

the father's requirements

ittle kids make little decisions—"Will I play in the sandbox or on the swing-set?" or "Should I pull Susie's hair or pinch her arm?" ▶ No big deal, right? ▶ Teens and young adults have it a whole lot tougher—"Should I go to college and if so, where?" "What job or career should I pursue?" "Should I get married and if so, to whom?" Those are the "biggies." ▶ Hey, guess what? God wants to help you make good decisions. And we want to show you some ways to tap into his wisdom. ▶ "I will instruct you and teach you in the way you should go; I will counsel you and watch over you" (Psalm 32:8).

It's No Secret

Can you relate to this? ❯ Grant is facing some big decisions—where to go to college, what to major in, if he and Susan have any sort of future—and he hasn't got the foggiest idea of what to do. He complains, "I want to do the right thing, but I'm so confused. I mean, I know God must have some sort of plan for my life, but for some reason, I can't figure out what it is. What if I make the wrong choices? What if I go in the wrong direction? It's kind of scary, because I don't want to end up regretting the decisions I make."

look it up —• There's no need to freak out over the what-should-I-do-type questions. Discovering God's will for your life is not like searching for buried treasure in the ocean. His will can be known.

Paul urged the Christians in Rome to "be transformed by the renewing of your mind. Then you will be able to test and approve what God's will is—his good, pleasing and perfect will" (Romans 12:2).

Paul also prayed for the believers in Colosse, "asking God to fill [them] with the knowledge of his will through all spiritual wisdom and understanding" (Colossians 1:9).

Obviously, Paul thought it was possible—and essential—to know God's will.

think it through —• Most parents are always giving their kids advice, telling them, "You need to do this" or "If I were in your shoes, I'd do that." Why? Usually because they love their kids and don't want them to make wrong choices.

In a much greater way God loves us and wants the best for us. Why then do we often think that he sits in heaven, tight-lipped and unwilling to give us guidance when we need it?

work it out —• Why not start off your study of God's will this week with a prayer:

"Father in heaven, thank you so much for loving me. Thank you for making your will for my life something that I can discover and not some impossible mystery. Teach me about the different ways you lead and guide your children as I look at your Word the next few days. You know I want my life to count for you. You know I want to do your will. Help me through Christ. Amen."

nail it down —• Read Psalm 143:10.

God's Will

As soon as 16-year-old Shelly graduates next May, she intends to marry her boyfriend, Will, who's 19. ◗ She's got it all planned. He'll keep working at his construction job. She'll enroll in beauty school. And they'll live happily ever after. ◗ There's one major problem. Shelly is a Christian and Will isn't. She argues, "But you don't really know Will. He's so sweet! And he promises that he'll come to church with me. I just know this is God's will. We really love each other. He'll become a Christian later."

look it up —• So much of God's will for our lives is already revealed—spelled out in the pages of the Bible.

- "God our Savior . . . wants all men to be saved and to come to a knowledge of the truth" (1 Timothy 2:3–4).

- "It is God's will that you should be sanctified: that you should avoid sexual immorality" (1 Thessalonians 4:3).

- "Be joyful always; pray continually; give thanks in all circumstances, for this is God's will for you in Christ Jesus" (1 Thessalonians 5:16–18).

think it through —• By carefully studying the commands and principles of God's Word, we can come up with a list of things that are clearly God's will for our lives. We might not find answers to specific questions like, "Which school should I attend?" but we can discover a lot of good, basic guidelines. (For instance, you never have to pray about whether God wants you to rob a bank.)

Based on 2 Corinthians 6:14–18, what is God's will for Shelly?

work it out —• Quickly read through Romans 12:9–21. Underline with pencil the commands in this passage.

These are not suggestions that you can take or leave. These requirements are the will of God for your life.

Determine that you will live according to these verses today and every day. If we don't follow the parts of God's will that he has already revealed to us in his Word, how much sense does it make to ask him to give us special guidance in other areas of life?

nail it down —• See more of God's will for your life in Ephesians 5.

pray about it —•

God's Will

3 Getting Guidance from God

group of Blaine's friends from Southside High are taking a senior trip to Florida. Blaine's pretty sure it's going to be a wild trip—in fact by the end of the week, almost the whole graduating class will be there. A couple of the guys going are Christian friends from church, but most of them aren't. ▶ Blaine feels torn. He wants to be with his friends. But at the same time, he doesn't want to go down there, get in a bunch of tempting situations, and blow his witness. ▶ How can he figure out what's best?

look it up —• Christians often overlook one of the best ways to discover God's will—simply talking to God in prayer.

When the Israelites entered Canaan, they were commanded to defeat and destroy all the inhabitants of the land. After a couple of victories, they encountered a group of people from nearby Gibeon who pretended to be from a faraway land. The Gibeonites' deception worked perfectly because "the men of Israel . . . did not inquire of the LORD. Then Joshua made a treaty of peace with [the Gibeonites] to let them live" (Joshua 9:14–15).

The point is this: By not seeking God's wisdom in complicated situations, we're asking for trouble.

think it through —• Many thousands of people write to newspaper advice columnists for direction. Often the counsel they get is superficial. Why do so many Christians fail to ask God for help in making decisions?

Do you think Christians may not talk to God about what to do because deep down they already know what's best? Is it possible Blaine feels this way?

work it out —• If you're facing a tough decision, you can't afford not to get God's wisdom. You need to talk things over with him . . . right now.

Like many things in the Christian faith, prayer is a mystery. But that doesn't mean it's impossible. God talks to us in his Word and world. He's designed prayer as the way we talk to him.

Present your situation to him, and ask him to reveal the best thing to do. Sooner or later, you'll get the answer you need (maybe not what you want, and maybe not the way you expect, but definitely what you need).

nail it down —• Read Philippians 4:6–7.

God's Will

4 C's for Charting Your Course

Jill has basically two goals in life: to develop her God-given artistic abilities and to reach people for Christ. Now, however, she's being forced to choose between two good opportunities. ▶ She's been offered a job at one of the leading art galleries in her city—a chance to learn new things and meet some talented, influential people. She's also just been given the opportunity to travel with a missionary team to Mexico. She'd love to do both, but if she goes to Mexico for three weeks, someone else will get the job in the gallery. ▶ Jill has three days to decide!

look it up —• Choosing between several good options is extremely tough. But you can discover the best option by evaluating these two C's:

- *Circumstances.* Realize there are no coincidences. God is in control of our lives and uses every incident to direct our steps. Investigate the various circumstances—spiritual, financial, emotional, social, physical—surrounding each option before deciding.
- *Counsel.* Don't neglect the wisdom of older, more mature Christians—your parents, pastor, teachers, youth workers. "Plans fail for lack of counsel, but with many advisers they succeed" (Proverbs 15:22).

think it through —• If your goal is to be a great drummer, but you have neither rhythm nor a drum set, your circumstances might be God's way of telling you that he has something else for you. If your minister keeps telling you, "God has given you some real gifts," maybe God is using such counsel to guide you.

But be careful! Circumstances can also make wrong choices look good. And some counsel, though meant for good, can be totally off base. Use these Cs cautiously and only after much prayer.

work it out —• On an index card, write down some tough choices you face today as well as "biggies" that loom on the horizon. Then take all the aspects of knowing God's will we've talked about so far and see if you can summarize them on another index card. The point is to develop a simple tool that you can carry around with you to help you make good decisions in tough situations.

If you're still unsure about which way to go, there are a few more tips tomorrow. Hang on.

nail it down —• Read Exodus 18:13–27.

pray about it —•

God's Will
63

5 Three More C's

- Stan has been accepted at two different schools—Freedom University and Einstein College. He has good friends going to each place. He likes certain things about each school. What should he do?
- Should Angela take a job at the clothing store or the dry cleaners? The pay is about the same.
- Curt can either play baseball or be in the spring play, but not both. He's both a good athlete and a gifted actor.

look it up —• Here are three more Cs to find God's will:

1. *Common Sense.* Christianity is a rational faith. God is a logical God. We're to love him with our minds, using our biblically informed reason in decision making. Paul often used common sense (Acts 15:38).

2. *Compulsion.* Often God gives us inner impressions to follow or not to follow a certain course. This was Paul's experience: "And now, compelled by the Spirit, I am going to Jerusalem" (Acts 20:22). Such leading is for us as well. "Those who are led by the Spirit of God are sons of God" (Romans 8:14). Remember, if you feel led, it's probably God. If you feel pressured, it's probably not.

3. *Contentment.* Being in God's will should result in an inner peace in our lives (Colossians 3:15).

think it through —• In light of the following facts, what would your counsel be? Stan found out that he doesn't have the money for Einstein College. Plus it doesn't offer the major he wants. Angela has been praying a lot and has a gut feeling that she ought to work at the clothing store. Curt, even though he's a good actor, doesn't enjoy drama nearly as much as baseball.

Again, be careful not to make decisions solely on these factors. Sometimes God asks his people to do things that seem illogical (Hosea 3:1). Sometimes inner impressions can mislead us. Sometimes his will isn't pleasant (Jonah 1:1–2). Always evaluate these C's in light of his Word.

work it out —• Because we've barely scratched the surface of figuring out what the Father wants, ask your youth pastor to recommend a book on knowing God's will.

Meanwhile, make sure you begin putting these introductory suggestions into practice. Start today.

nail it down —• Read Ephesians 5:17. Use your devotional times this weekend to memorize this short verse.

God's Will

topic

Media

mass communication or mass manipulation?

Newspapers, magazines, books, radio, television, movies—not one of us goes a day without exposure to some form of mass communication. If we're not careful about what we read, hear, and watch, we can be subtly manipulated. That's because many nonbiblical messages are being communicated. ❱ For a look at some of the ways the media influence us, meet Derek, Amy, Chris, Kelley, and Walter—members of the Pratt Academy Media Club. ❱ "Finally, brothers, whatever is true, whatever is noble, whatever is right, whatever is pure, whatever is lovely, whatever is admirable—if anything is excellent or praiseworthy—think about such things" (Philippians 4:8).

Blood and Guts

et's meet our first Media Club member: ▶ Derek Dillard, age 16. Distinction: Most horror flicks seen by any teenager east of Death Valley. Aspiration: To be the next Stephen King. ▶ "Gory stuff doesn't bug me," Derek brags. "I've got a cast-iron stomach." ▶ He's seen the entire *Nightmare on Elm Street* series (he's even got a "Freddy" poster on his wall) and every installment of *Friday the 13th* at least twice. His all-time favorite is *Halloween.* ▶ Claims Derek, "Nothing beats a plate of nachos and a good horror flick on Saturday night."

look it up —• Does the Bible have a word for Derek (and for us)? You'd better believe it.

- "Do not envy a violent man or choose any of his ways, for the LORD detests a perverse man but takes the upright into his confidence" (Proverbs 3:31–32).

- "From the fruit of his lips a man enjoys good things, but the unfaithful have a craving for violence" (Proverbs 13:2).

- "The violence of the wicked will drag them away, for they refuse to do what is right" (Proverbs 21:7).

It doesn't take an Einstein to look at these verses and realize that God disapproves of violence— and that includes the violence portrayed in the media.

think it through —• Lately Derek has become insensitive to violence; it just doesn't bother him anymore. The other day he watched two guys beat up a classmate after school. His reaction was, "That's life!"

If you think constant exposure to "blood and guts" (even if it's all fake) doesn't affect people, how do you respond to the numerous studies that conclusively link media violence with aggressive, hostile behavior?

work it out —• Take action against the violence in your life! Make a list of movies and bands you know of that glamorize or focus on violence. How many of these movies and bands are part of your regular media diet? Knowing God's perspective on violence, are you willing to turn your attention somewhere else?

Copy Philippians 4:8 on an index card and carry it around with you this week. Memorize it and make it a goal in your life.

nail it down —• Read about God's judgment on violent behavior in Genesis 6:11–13.

Media

2 Glamour Zines

Amy Kramer, age 15. Aspiration: To become the editor-in-chief of *Vogue* magazine. ▶ Pick a popular women's magazine and Amy—or one of her friends—subscribes to it. *Glamour, Vogue, Seventeen, Elle, . . .* the girls swap them all. ▶ Night after night they call each other to discuss new trends in the fashion industry. ▶ "Jill, did you see that dress by Versace on page 103 of *Glamour?* I'm dying!" ▶ "I know. I'd give anything just to wear it one night!"

look it up —• What's the problem? Well, the more the girls look, the more they want. And the more they want, the more discontent they grow because they can't afford all those things. So they spend their days (and nights) wishing for new clothes, hating the "rotten" things they have to wear, and growing more resentful.

They need to pay attention to these words of Jesus:

"Watch out! Be on your guard against all kinds of greed; a man's life does not consist in the abundance of his possessions" (Luke 12:15).

think it through —• Looking at magazines is not sinful. But realize that publishers of many fashion magazines (and mail order catalogs too) have one supreme objective. Each wants to convince you that you *need* the products advertised within its pages. The ads are designed to appeal to the base elements of lust, vanity, and greed within all of us. And unfortunately, the results are very effective.

work it out —• In the chart below, list the magazines you read regularly. Grade each one on a scale of 1–10 (1 means it conveys a worldly outlook; 10 means it adopts a biblical perspective):

	Magazine	Rating
1.	_____	_____
2.	_____	_____
3.	_____	_____
4.	_____	_____

Based on your conclusions above, should you alter your reading habits? Make the commitment now to cut any negative influences out of your life.

nail it down —• Read Ephesians 5:3.

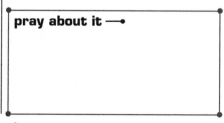

pray about it —•

3 Steamy Scenes

Our third media expert is Chris Noll, 17. Aspiration: To photograph beautiful (and scantily clad) women for a living. ▶ He spends much of his time looking at bodies—in movies, in the *Sports Illustrated* swimsuit issue, or on the Playboy channel. ▶ But Chris has a problem. He can't get the gorgeous bodies he's seen out of his mind—even when he wants to. Like during his algebra test. Or in church. Or when he's trying to go to sleep at night.

look it up —• The human body is a beautiful creation of God. He did not intend it to be exploited in immodest display. Jesus clearly stated, "'I tell you that anyone who looks at a woman lustfully has already committed adultery with her in his heart'" (Matthew 5:28).

Why is lust so improper for believers? Because "those who belong to Christ Jesus have crucified the sinful nature with its passions and desires" (Galatians 5:24).

think it through —• According to both the Bible and the testimonies of those who have been controlled by lust, activities involving porn movies or magazines are far from harmless. Lust is an enslaving, addictive force that is *never* satisfied. It always wants more.

Media producers and ad executives fully understand this. That's why they fill their TV shows, movies, commercials, and songs with erotic images. We grow increasingly frustrated as they grow increasingly rich.

work it out —• Quickly list what you've seen, heard, and read in the last week. Include

- that steamy miniseries on television
- your weekend movie rentals
- radio talk shows
- MTV
- trashy romance novels and glossy skin magazines

Are those really the kinds of images that you want to fill your mind with?

Say no to lust. Forget those destructive activities and fill your time with healthy pursuits. Find a friend who will struggle with you to keep body and mind pure in an impure world.

nail it down —• Read Psalm 8:4–5.

elley Masterson, 16, is distinguished by her familiarity with soap operas. Aspiration: To direct a daytime soap. ❱ *All My Children. The Young and the Restless. The Idle and the Depraved.* Kelley keeps up with them all. ❱ Kelley's a Christian who grew up believing that abortion and divorce are wrong. But now as she watches more soaps, and spends less time in God's Word, she wonders, "Maybe abortion is the best thing if a girl is unmarried and pregnant. I'm not sure I could stay married to the same person for life."

look it up —• As the Israelites prepared to enter the Promised Land, God's concern was that they not become infected with pagan values. Time and again, he warned the people to live according to his Word, not according to the world:

"Be careful, or you will be enticed to turn away and worship other gods and bow down to them. . . . Fix these words of mine in your hearts and minds. . . .

"See that you do all I command you; do not add to it or take away from it" (Deuteronomy 11:16, 18; 12:32).

think it through —• What you see, hear, and read in the media is never free of bias. Every producer, writer, or director has some philosophy of life that colors his or her work—no matter how objective each tries to be. In fact, a study by the research team of Lichter and Rothman indicates that the most powerful figures in media are extremely antagonistic to biblical values!

work it out —• Are you hooked on the intrigue, suspense, and excitement of the soaps? Do you love being shocked by the schemes of some soap opera vixen? Try something different.

Turn off your TV tonight and pick up the Bible. Read the book of Judges. It will take you less than an hour. There won't be any cliffhangers. Your values won't be challenged by the denial of absolute morality. Devious men and women won't be portrayed as winners.

Judges paints a true picture of the suffering that sin causes. No exaggeration—you'll never find a soap opera as exciting or true-to-life as this book of the Bible. See for yourself!

nail it down —• Read Romans 12:2.

pray about it —•

5 Is All Spirituality Good?

Here's one last close-up of a member of the Pratt Academy Media Club: ▶ Walter Waugh, 14, is a sci-fi genius. Aspiration: To write a science fiction series and produce it into several blockbuster movies. ▶ Walter's not very popular but what does he care? He's got his hands full reading sci-fi novels, seeing fantasy movies, and dabbling in psychic phenomena. ▶ Yesterday he sat for a full hour staring at a piece of paper balanced on a pencil, determined to move the paper with his mind. It didn't work. But he'll keep trying.

look it up —• More movies and TV shows than ever before are exploring various forms of spirituality. But not everything "spiritual" is Christian. Don't let talk about spirits, angels, or even prayer fool you into accepting what's being said without examining it closely. The Bible gives this warning:

"See to it that no one takes you captive through hollow and deceptive philosophy, which depends on human tradition and the basic principles of this world rather than on Christ" (Colossians 2:8).

Though it claims to put people in touch with God and themselves, much of the spirituality expressed in the media is deceptive.

think it through —• On a website promoting Wicca (a contemporary form of witchcraft), a writer suggested that one reason Wicca is growing in popularity with teenagers is that shows like *Buffy the Vampire Slayer, Charmed, Bewitched*, and *Sabrina the Teenage Witch* have improved public perception of witches by their positive portrayals. Even people who don't take the shows seriously are subtly influenced to view witchcraft as harmless or acceptable. The same holds true for other offbeat brands of spirituality endorsed in other shows.

work it out —• Does that mean you should never watch a show or go to a movie unless you're sure you know what kind of spirituality it's promoting? Well, that might not be a bad idea. At the very least, don't turn off your brain when you sit down in front of the screen. Many people do just that. They get so caught up in how a movie looks ("It's so amazing! You'll laugh your head off!") that often they don't realize the dangerous messages being presented at the same time.

Be discerning when it comes to entertainment:

- Keep a sharp lookout today for the unbiblical ideas that are so common in the media.
- See if you can isolate two or three statements or ideas that are being communicated that are clearly wrong.

nail it down —• Read Hebrews 13:9 on Saturday; on Sunday read 2 Timothy 4:3–4.

The Great Debate

Teenager No. 1: "Well, I think they've sold out. They're big stars now, but only because they leave Jesus out of their songs."

Teenager No. 2: "Are you kidding? They haven't sold out! They've just sold CDs to people who otherwise wouldn't buy Christian music. What's wrong with that?"

The Great Christian Music Debate: Because of the "secular" success of some well-known Christian artists, a lot of Christian teens (and adults) have had some version of the above conversation.

And though I know you may disagree, I'm going to take sides. In my opinion, Teenager No. 2—the one defending Christian artists who do songs not explicitly about Jesus—has the better argument. Here's why:

Music Is Not Only for Evangelism: Who ever said that music has to be evangelistic to be moral? As far as I know, God hasn't. There is no Bible verse I can think of that forbids musical expression of other themes besides explicitly religious ones.

A Question of Perspective: Christian artists and musicians must approach their work from the perspective of truth, of course. But a truthful perspective encompasses *all* of God's creation. It's not limited to the church only.

That's why Christian architects do more than design churches. They design churches, office buildings, libraries, banks, and more—with the intent of glorifying God with their work. That's why Christian teachers teach other subjects besides theology. They teach theology, history, math, science, and physical education—with the intent of glorifying God with their work.

How could it be wrong for P.O.D. to sing a song about our nation's youth? Or Sixpence None the Richer to sing innocent songs such as "Kiss Me" and "There She Goes"?

Drawing the Line: There is a line, of course. It is *never* moral to use art to glorify a false philosophy or to condone sinful behavior—regardless of the reason. If P.O.D. were to sing about how great violence is, and then try to justify it as a way to reach troubled teens, they would be guilty of a terrible sin. But as long as this new breed of crossover Christian artists are looking out on the world from the perspective of truth (Philippians 4:8), I say bravo!

That's one editor's viewpoint. Maybe you could see it that way too.

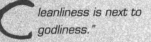

Statements you Won't Find in the Bible

C leanliness is next to
godliness."

The statement is reputed to have
come from the ancient writings of
the Hebrew rabbis. John Wesley, the
founder of the Methodist Church, is
also known to have said this.

"The Devil made me do it."

This is commonly heard when people
do something naughty. Though Satan
does tempt us and does try to
destroy us, he has no power to make
us do anything. We can only point
the finger at ourselves.

*"I am god. You are god. We are all
god."*

*"If you wish to find god, look within
yourself, for he is part of all of us."*

Statements like these are becoming
more common as New Age thought
(that is, Eastern mysticism)
becomes more and more popular in
this country.

God is not all. He is omnipresent, yet
distinct from his creation.

God is not within all. He dwells in his
children (John 1:12). Unlike the life-
force god of the New Agers, the one
true God is personal and knowable.

"Money is the root of all evil."

What the Bible really says is that "the
love of money is a root of all kinds of
evil" (1 Timothy 6:10).

*"There is no right or wrong—just
what works for you."*

"Go with the flow."

"If it feels good, do it."

*"There are no absolutes—everything
is relative."*

All of these slogans, part of the
"bumper-sticker philosophy" in this
country, may be attributed to a secular mindset that resists authority and
values personal freedom and the pur-
suit of pleasure. You won't find any of
these in the Bible.

 topic ———————————————————

Forgiveness

not the way of the world

When you're 25 or 50 or 75, you may not remember much about this devotional. But if you forget everything else, please at least try to grasp the thoughts discussed in the next few pages. ▶ Take your time. Read carefully. Think clearly. Pray intensely. Discuss earnestly. Because the truths you are about to study have the potential to change you forever. No kidding . . . they can be the difference between an okay life and an incredible one. ▶ Which one sounds better to you? ▶ "In him we have redemption through his blood, the forgiveness of sins, in accordance with the riches of God's grace" (Ephesians 1:7).

Your Debt Has Been Paid in Full

At Bible study, Ashley and Michael heard this: "Because of sin, the entire human race is under a death sentence. But Jesus came and paid the penalty for sin by dying in our place. If you trust him, you can experience total forgiveness. ❱ "Forgiveness isn't based on anything you do to earn it. It's based on what Jesus has already done. He paid for your sins. Now the question is: Will you accept that payment?" ❱ Ashley said yes. Michael said no. He figured, "That can't be right! Surely, God must expect me to do something to make up for my sins."

look it up ─● The book of Acts tells how the followers of Christ went all over the known world with the message of forgiveness:

- "All the prophets testify about him that everyone who believes in him receives forgiveness of sins through his name" (Acts 10:43).

- "Therefore, my brothers, I want you to know that through Jesus the forgiveness of sins is proclaimed to you" (Acts 13:38).

No wonder they were excited: Jesus completely paid the debt we could never pay!

think it through ─● You break the law and are caught. Because of your crime, the judge fines you $1,000. What are you going to do? You deserve to be punished. Yet you don't have the money to pay the penalty.

Suddenly, the judge pulls out his checkbook, and pays the fine you owe. Your debt to society has been canceled. Your offense is forgiven.

God has done that for us on an infinitely grander scale. The very payment he demanded for sin—death—he has supplied through his Son.

work it out ─● If you've already experienced forgiveness through Christ, tell God how thankful you are. Then tell someone else.

If you're not sure, you can be by sincerely praying: "God, I know I've sinned. I need and want to be forgiven. Right now, I am trusting Jesus to be my Savior. I believe the message of the Bible—that his death on the cross paid the penalty for all my sins. Amen."

nail it down ─● Read Acts 2:38.

Forgiveness

Stop the Reruns

wo years ago, during their sophomore year, Michael and Ashley went out for about four months. The relationship had gotten extremely physical when suddenly, for no apparent reason, Michael stopped calling Ashley. Hurt and confused, Ashley could not understand why Michael would not return her phone calls. As she tried to work through the pain and guilt, she said, "I guess God is punishing me for what I did. Even if he forgives me, I'm not sure that I can ever forgive myself."

look it up —• Refusing to forgive ourselves when God says he's forgiven us makes no sense. It's like saying that we know more about dealing with sin than God does. Notice that he not only forgives, he also forgets:

- "I have swept away your offenses like a cloud, your sins like the morning mist" (Isaiah 44:22).

- "As far as the east is from the west, so far has he removed our transgressions from us" (Psalm 103:12).

- "You will tread our sins underfoot and hurl all our iniquities into the depths of the sea" (Micah 7:19).

think it through —• Every time we really determine to walk with God or serve him, the Devil starts playing reruns of all our sins and whispering, "You're no good. God could never use a sinner like you."

Maybe this explains why Ashley was like a spiritual yo-yo for almost a year. How should she have responded in light of God's promised forgiveness?

work it out —• If you can't forgive yourself for certain actions, pray: "God, though you say I am totally forgiven, I realize I have never forgiven myself for _____. Right now I choose to believe what you say, and also to forgive myself. Once and for all, I ask you to lift that burden from me and release me from my guilt."

The next time Satan brings up sins from your past, fight back with the Word of God. He will not be able to stand against you or tell you lies when you pull out your spiritual sword.

- "Who is he that condemns? Christ Jesus ... who was raised to life ... is also interceding for us" (Romans 8:34).

- "The one who is in you is greater than the one who is in the world" (1 John 4:4).

nail it down —• Read Isaiah 43:25.

pray about it —•

Forgiveness

3 Forgiveness Is for Giving

Up until a month ago, Ashley could not stand even the thought of Michael. Though they had broken up over two years ago, she still felt angry about their whole experience. She felt used and mistreated. ▶ To get back, she avoided Michael at school. And any time he came to youth group activities, she ignored him. "Until he apologizes for what he did to me, I'll never even speak to him." ▶ Four weeks ago something happened. Ashley's preacher talked about forgiveness. Ashley hasn't been the same since.

look it up —• The following facts prompted the change in Ashley's attitude:

- God has forgiven us for all the wrong things we have done (Psalm 103:3).

- Because God has forgiven us, we must forgive others. "Bear with each other and forgive whatever grievances you may have against one another. Forgive as the Lord forgave you" (Colossians 3:13).

- Our fellowship with God is interrupted when we refuse to forgive others. "For if you forgive men when they sin against you, your heavenly Father will also forgive you. But if you do not forgive men their sins, your Father will not forgive your sins" (Matthew 6:14–15).

think it through —• Forgiveness is not

- denying that you've been hurt;

- explaining away the wrong behavior of someone;

- trying to understand why a person has acted a certain way.

Forgiveness is consciously choosing to release others from debts we feel they owe us because of hurts they have caused us.

Whom in your life do you need to forgive?

work it out —• You can experience the freedom Ashley found by praying:

"God, I am angry and hurt because of what _____ has done to me. I don't feel like forgiving, and in my own strength I know I can't. But because you have completely forgiven me, right now I choose to forgive _____ for _____. Today, by your grace, I will begin accepting _____, and I will seek to rebuild our broken fellowship."

nail it down —• Read Matthew 18:23–35.

Forgiveness

4 Does God Need Our Forgiveness?

When Ashley understood God's forgiveness, she began her spiritual journey. Learning to forgive herself was her first obstacle, but in time she was back on track. She took another giant step by realizing the need to forgive others—especially Michael. ▶ The other day Ashley was telling a friend some of the things she's been learning. When the subject of forgiveness came up, her friend exploded. "God forgive *me?* If anything, I need to be forgiving him! Why did he let my dad die when I was only two? How could he?"

look it up ⟶ People understandably question God when life gets rough. King David was no exception:

"My God, my God, why have you forsaken me? Why are you so far from saving me? . . . O my God, I cry out by day, but you do not answer, by night, and am not silent" (Psalm 22:1–2).

For David, relief finally came when he remembered God's perfection and his faithfulness (Psalm 22:4–5). That's how we should respond too.

think it through ⟶ In his best-selling book, *When Bad Things Happen to Good People,* Rabbi Harold Kushner suggests that we need to forgive God for being unable to prevent bad experiences from entering our lives.

Such an idea is blasphemous! God is perfect and needs no forgiveness—he cannot sin against us. But we live in a fallen world, where our sin has allowed disease, hatred, violence, and other miseries to enter. As long as God gives us free will, we are going to be free to decide to sin . . . and to suffer the consequences.

work it out ⟶ If you're holding a grudge against God for letting suffering into your life, you might want to pray something like this:

"Lord, I feel angry at you because of _____. I admit that I've been prideful and stubborn, believing that I know better than you what's best for me. Right now I give up my angry demands for an explanation. I willingly accept the circumstances you have allowed in my life. I choose to trust you. Keep reminding me that you are totally wise and completely good. Amen."

nail it down ⟶ See Jeremiah's anger at God—Jeremiah 20:7–18.

pray about it ⟶

What Happens If I Refuse to Forgive?

5

Ashley went to have lunch after church with a new girl named Jean Marie. Eventually the small talk turned into a serious conversation. ▶ "That was really good, that stuff you said about forgiving others," the newcomer sighed. "I guess I should feel that way too . . . but there's no way." Jean Marie's eyes filled with tears. "I can never forgive my stepfather for all the wrong things he's done to me." She burst out crying, "I hate him so much! I pray every night that he'll die!"

look it up ──• Bitterness hurts us far more than it will ever harm anyone else. The story of Saul is a sober reminder of this fact. He became bitter because the people praised David more than they did him:

"As they danced, they sang: 'Saul has slain his thousands, and David his tens of thousands.' Saul was very angry; this refrain galled him. . . . And from that time on Saul kept a jealous eye on David" (1 Samuel 18:7–9).

From that point, Saul's life was downhill. He grew insecure, violent, and irrational. Because he never dealt with his bitterness, his life ended in ruin and disgrace.

think it through ──• One pastor has summed up the danger of an unforgiving spirit like this: "It is like a hot coal. The longer and tighter it is held, the deeper the burn. Like a hot coal, bitterness too will leave a scar that even time cannot erase."

Remember, forgiveness does not mean that you must entirely forget what happened. It does not mean that you will immediately cease to feel hurt. But you must forgive your "debtors" before God can begin to heal you of that hurt.

work it out ──• No matter how deeply or how often you have suffered because of someone else, you *can* be freed from an unforgiving spirit.

- List all the ways you feel you have been wronged.

- Remember that God has forgiven you and that he expects you to forgive others.

- Confess your bitter attitude as sin (others can't make you bitter—bitterness is a choice).

- When appropriate, talk with the individual(s) involved, confess your bitter attitude, and ask for forgiveness.

nail it down ──• Think about Hebrews 12:15 on Friday. On Saturday and Sunday memorize Ephesians 4:32.

Forgiveness

 topic ————————————————————————

Stress

coping with the pressures of life

You have an eight-page paper due tomorrow, and you haven't started it yet. ▶ Tryouts are next week, but you don't know when you'll have a minute to focus on what it will take to succeed. ▶ Your friend's dad just lost his job and may move his family out of state to find work. You and your friend are both miserable about it. ▶ You saw the most popular girl in the class cheating on the last history test. She knows you saw her and has been putting the pressure on you not to tell. ▶ You can probably add a half dozen more stressful events to this list. Let's face it: stress is a fact of life for most teens. ▶ Does God have anything to say on the subject? Keep reading for biblical insight on how to cope in a pressure-packed world. ▶ "But I call to God, and the LORD saves me. Evening, morning and noon I cry out in distress, and he hears my voice" (Psalm 55:16–17).

Learning to Share the Load

Seventeen-year-old Adrienne is on the verge of losing it. Last year her mother suddenly left home and is living with some guy in Idaho. Now, on top of her studies, part-time job, and involvement in a couple of groups at school and church, Adrienne has the added pressure of being a stand-in mom to her little sister while her dad works an extra job. ▶ Yesterday when she got an English paper back with a big red D on it, she dissolved in tears. ▶ "Adrienne, get a grip! It's just one paper," urged Judi. ▶ "You don't understand!" Adrienne sobbed.

look it up —• You don't have to live in a broken home to feel the pressure of responsibility. That kind of stress is everywhere. Consider the advice Moses got when he was worn out from settling the disputes of the people:

"What you are doing is not good. . . . The work is too heavy for you; you cannot handle it alone" (Exodus 18:17–18).

The speaker was Jethro, Moses' father-in-law. He urged the exhausted leader of Israel to find some helpers. "That will make your load lighter, because they will share it with you. If you do this and God so commands, you will be able to stand the strain" (vv. 22–23).

think it through —• How can you tell when the stress levels in your life are too high? Any of the following may be warning signals: nervousness, depression, irritability, sleeping difficulty, change in appetite (not eating at all or binge eating), headaches, fatigue, frequent crying, inability to concentrate, skin problems, or apathy.

work it out —• If you feel stressed beyond your limit, seek out others who can help lighten your load.

- Find a prayer partner during especially stressful periods.

- Look for a study buddy in your hardest class.

- Confide in a close friend during painful times.

- Pour out your heart to a parent or youth leader when you feel weary.

- Ask a brother or sister for help in completing tough tasks.

Why try to carry burdens that are too heavy for one person? The body of Christ is there to help you. But you first have to ask for help!

nail it down —• Memorize Galatians 6:2.

Louis Watkins is as nervous as a long-tailed cat in a room full of rocking chairs. On Saturday he takes the SAT test for the third time. His parents want him to improve his scores radically. ▶ Each night they remind him how important it is that he study. "You need at least a 1350 or 1400, Lou!" Mr. Watkins insists (for about the two-hundredth time). "Make us proud, son. No goofing off till after this weekend, okay?" ▶ Lou nods weakly, his stomach in knots. He hates to think what will happen if he disappoints his parents.

look it up —• Have you ever battled extreme pressure? Have you ever felt so tense you wondered how you would be able to function? If so, you're not alone. Consider this charge given to Israel:

"When you go to war against your enemies ... do not be afraid.... Do not be fainthearted or afraid; do not be terrified or give way to panic before them. For the LORD your God is the one who goes with you to fight for you against your enemies to give you victory" (Deuteronomy 20:1, 3–4).

What a promise! The pressure for success isn't on you. It's on God. Your obligation is simply to "go to war." It's up to God to give you the victory.

think it through —• How would you handle the stress if you had parents like Lou? Is it right for parents to put that much pressure on their children? Is it right for us to put that much pressure on ourselves?

work it out —• Don't lose the biblical perspective. When your back is to the wall, all you have to do is your part. What is your part in the stresses you face?

• In academics, your part is to study.

• In a conflict involving a relationship, your part is to apologize and be kind.

• In athletics, your part is to be in shape.

• In a tempting situation, your part is to turn away from sin.

• In a pressure-filled job, your part is to work hard and be cheerful.

Once you know your part, simply do your part. Then give the pressure to God. He can handle it. (He can also bring victory ... when we trust him.)

nail it down —• Read Isaiah 63:7–9.

pray about it —•

Talk to God during Stress's Mess

3

What would you feel like doing in the following situations?

- Biff Hooper, the biggest senior on the football team, has vowed to beat the you-know-what out of Tommy for giving his girlfriend a ride home.
- Carla Maddox has been wrongly accused of cheating during a history exam.
- Melinda just learned that her father is being transferred. She'll be moving away from the town she's lived in all her life.
- David Pearce, who has a mortal fear of speaking to large groups, has to give an oral report in class tomorrow.

look it up —• No matter what you're facing, remember the stressful experience of David in Psalm 18:

First, David prayed. "In my distress I called to the LORD; I cried to my God for help" (v. 6).

Second, God answered. "From his temple he heard my voice; my cry came before him, into his ears" (v. 6).

Turning to God was David's immediate response. On the heels of another tense occasion, David proclaimed: "Surely God is my help; the Lord is the one who sustains me.... For he has deliv-

ered me from all my troubles" (Psalm 54:4, 7).

think it through —• The words to an old hymn underscore the truth that prayer is the best response to stress:

I must tell Jesus all of my trials.
I cannot bear these burdens alone.
In my distress He kindly will save me.
He always loves and cares for His own.

That one little stanza contains a lot of truth, doesn't it?

work it out —• Some people, when facing a stressful situation, do everything but pray. They toss and turn, agonize, plan, scheme, fret, connive, plot, consult friends, worry, calculate, and finally trust in their own abilities to overcome the pressure. Why not just turn all the headaches over to God—right off the bat?

Here's what we're talking about: "Lord, I feel really stressed out because of _____. I don't know what to do. I'm tired and scared. The problem is too big for me to handle. Please take control of the situation. Give me your peace. Keep reminding me that you will take care of things. Amen."

nail it down —• Read Psalm 4:1.

Stress

4 Stress Can Result in the Best

Remember Melinda? The girl who had to move from her hometown? Well, nine months later, she's finally beginning to see that the situation may not be so horrible after all. She says, "The move was so hard. We were all totally depressed at first. But what could we do? We had to lean on each other—and especially on God. ❱ "I still miss my friends. But I'm meeting some great people at my new school and actually starting to like this place. My family is closer, and God is a bigger part of our lives now."

look it up —• It's important to remember that since God is in control, stressful circumstances can have positive results. For example, stress can

- bring about real character in our lives: "When he has tested me, I will come forth as gold" (Job 23:10);

- cause us to have a closer walk with Christ (2 Corinthians 12:7–10);

- provide opportunities for us to be good examples to others: "In spite of severe suffering, you welcomed the message with the joy given by the Holy Spirit. And so you became a model to all the believers in Macedonia and Achaia" (1 Thessalonians 1:6–7);

- result in future reward: "For our light and momentary troubles are achieving for us an eternal glory that far outweighs them all" (2 Corinthians 4:17).

think it through —• Consider how hard times produce character. Do you turn to Christ when the pressures rise in your life? In your most recent stressful situation, how good an example were you to others? God really does give future glory for those who patiently endure present difficulties.

work it out —• If you find yourself cornered by stress right now, stop focusing on your negative circumstances. Try these three steps:

1. Ask God to show you the positive aspects of your situation. There are always *some*.

2. Memorize one of the verses cited in today's Look It Up section.

3. Quote that verse to yourself every time you are tempted to forget that God is in control of the stress in your life.

nail it down —• Read Romans 8:28.

pray about it —•

Last week was full of stress for Helen Williams. ❱ On Monday she waited to receive her term paper. She had put off the assignment until the night before it was due. The grade wouldn't be good. ❱ On Wednesday Helen dreaded bumping into Martha Porter. Helen had made a rude remark about Martha, Martha found out, and Helen feared a showdown. ❱ Friday night, at a party, Helen yielded to the influence of friends who were saying, "Have a drink—loosen up!" Later that same night in the car, Rob pressured Helen with a similar message.

look it up —• Have you ever considered that many of the stresses we face, we really bring on ourselves? Such pressures can be avoided by following two biblical principles:

1. Alter your lifestyle and become more disciplined. "Be very careful, then, how you live—not as unwise but as wise, making the most of every opportunity, because the days are evil" (Ephesians 5:15–16).

2. Avoid certain situations altogether—"Flee the evil desires of youth, and pursue righteousness, faith, love and peace, along with those who call on the Lord out of a pure heart" (2 Timothy 2:22).

think it through —• What, if anything, could Helen have done to eliminate the stresses she felt regarding the term paper? The Martha Porter incident? The temptations she faced on Friday night?

What can you learn from her mistakes to avoid having to go through similar stresses yourself?

work it out —• Eliminate some future stress today by doing one or more of the following:

• Begin working ahead on a big school assignment. Do some advance research for an upcoming paper or start reading that big novel for English.

• Bite your tongue when tempted to say something negative about someone. (Such comments almost always come back to haunt us and create tension in our relationships.)

• Refuse invitations to go places where you know you'll face incredible peer pressure.

nail it down —• Read Psalm 20:1–4. On Saturday read the rest of Psalm 20. On Sunday read 2 Chronicles 20:1–30.

WORD POWER

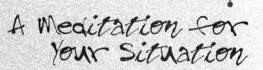

A Meditation for Your Situation

ere's where to look in the Bible if you're:

- Struggling with recurring sin—Romans 6:1–14.
- In need of forgiveness—Psalms 32 and 51.
- Wondering if God really loves you—Romans 8:31–39.
- Feeling weak or tired—Isaiah 40:29–31.
- Having trouble trusting God—Psalm 37.
- Asking, "Why do the wicked prosper?"—Psalm 73.

- Trying to understand what faith is—Hebrews 11.
- Forgetting how precious you are to God—Ephesians 1:3–14.
- Not getting along with others—Colossians 3:12–17.
- Looking for motivation to live for Christ—2 Corinthians 5:11–21.
- Questioning what heaven is like—Revelation 21–22.
- Wrestling with peer pressure—Romans 12.
- Afraid—Isaiah 41:10.

Angels

I believe in guardian angels," Gretchen said with complete confidence. "There's no other explanation." Gretchen's certainty about the angelic world is based on a horrifying experience she had as a young mother. Returning home from shopping one day, she turned her car into a busy intersection. Suddenly, the passenger door flung open and Joel, her three-year-old son, tumbled onto the highway! Gretchen screamed, and to her horror saw that a car was barreling directly for her son!

But as fast as the incident had happened, Joel was back in the car, sitting in the seat. There wasn't a scratch on him. And there wasn't a natural explanation possible. Shaking uncontrollably, Gretchen pulled over, bowed her head, and thanked God that his angels watched over her son that day.

Do Angels Exist? God's Word is unmistakably clear: Thirty-four of the sixty-six books of the Bible contain specific references to angels. Jesus himself affirmed the reality of these creatures (Mark 13:27, 32).

Where Do Angels Come From? Contrary to popular opinion, angels are not people who have died, gone to heaven, and "earned their wings" by performing especially good deeds. They are a special class of spirit beings created by God to serve him

(Psalm 148:2–5; Colossians 1:16). As spiritual beings, angels have spiritual bodies. And yet Scripture indicates that angels can appear in human form (Genesis 18 and 19).

Angels Are Busy? Angels are depicted in the Bible as God's ministers of divine work and worship. They are involved in worshiping God (Isaiah 6:3) and they serve as personal messengers from God to humans. In Old Testament times they led the Israelites out of Egypt and fought for and protected them during their wanderings.

Angels also had a major role in New Testament times. They predicted and celebrated the birth of Christ (Luke 1:26–33; 2:8–14). They ministered to Jesus after his temptation and during his passion (Matthew 4:11; Luke 22:43). They announced Christ's resurrection and ascension (Matthew 28:2–7; Acts 1:10–11). They delivered Peter from prison (Acts 5:17–20). Angelic beings also protect believers and minister to them (Hebrews 1:14).

Met Any Angels Lately? While we may wonder at these marvelous beings, we must never worship them (Colossians 2:18). And we must be friendly to strangers too . . . "For by so doing some people have entertained angels without knowing it" (Hebrews 13:2).

Origins

where did it all begin?

W*here did the universe come from?* ▶ *How did life originate?* ▶ These are, without doubt, two of the most profound questions we can ask. ▶ And when we strip away all the facts, data, and opposing theories, there are but two possible answers to each query: ▶ *1. Incredible luck.* ▶ *2. Intricate engineering.*

What Was There in the Beginning?

In science class, Eileen is being exposed to the latest theories about the origin of the universe. ▶ "Students, some scientists believe the Big Bang theory—that the cosmos suddenly exploded into existence, by chance, about 15 billion years ago. Others, like Stephen Hawking of Cambridge University, think the universe has always existed. ▶ "Those are the only two rational possibilities."

look it up —• Without chemical details, mentions of atomic theory, descriptions of pulsars, or precise dates, the Bible states another option:

"In the beginning God created the heavens and the earth" (Genesis 1:1).

Someone has suggested that the reason for this lack of technical information is that the Bible wasn't written as a science textbook. It's primarily a revelation from God about how we can know him.

So while it doesn't answer every little question about origins, the Bible does answer the big one. "The universe is not the product of blind chance. And it hasn't always existed. It was specially created by God."

think it through —• Follow this reasoning:

- **Anything that comes into existence must have a cause.** This is the scientific principle of causality.

- **The universe came into existence.**

The second law of thermodynamics (the fact that the universe is running out of energy and moving toward disorder) and the rapid expansion of the universe suggest it had an initial point of beginning.

Noted scientists Allen Sandage and Robert Jastrow have examined this and other evidence and concluded that the universe must have had a beginning.

- **Therefore, the universe must have a cause.**

work it out —• Is the debate over origins important to our faith? Most definitely. Can origins be explained simply and in the spaces of five devotional pages? Not a chance.

All the more reason to pray: "Father, at least, give me a good, general grasp of the main issues this week so that I can withstand the attacks on my faith that are sure to come. Amen."

nail it down —• Read Genesis 1.

Origins

The Foolish Premise of Evolution

2

ileen wants to believe the Bible is true, but the pro-evolution lectures she's getting in science class are messing with her mind. Plus she's getting hit from two additional sources:

- She subscribes to *National Geographic*, which constantly refers to evolution and the universe, but never mentions God.
- Her boyfriend says the idea of Creation is a joke. He says evolution disproves the Bible—and God.

look it up —• Evolution is disturbing, not just from a scientific perspective, but also from a theological point of view. Why is that? Well, in its purest form, the theory of evolution is atheistic. It opposes any belief in a Divine Creator. Note what God's Word says about such a philosophy:

- "In his pride the wicked does not seek him; in all his thoughts there is no room for God" (Psalm 10:4).

- "The fool says in his heart, 'There is no God'" (Psalm 14:1).

- "Since the creation of the world God's invisible qualities ... have been clearly seen, being understood from what has been made, so that men are without excuse" (Romans 1:20).

The inevitable conclusion is this: Creationism and the Darwinian theory of evolution cannot be reconciled.

think it through —• How can so many people look at our complex cosmos and conclude that God doesn't exist?

Romans 1:18–20 gives us the answer. This passage describes how people reject God's revelation of himself in nature. In short, these people "suppress the truth." All the evidence in the world (and there is a vast amount) isn't sufficient to convince them.

work it out —• Take an hour today to observe the universe around you. Lie down in some quiet place and look up at the clouds, trees, birds, and blue sky. Shut your eyes and listen to the sounds. Absorb the smells.

Finally, end your devotional time thinking about the great mystery of the universe. Praise the Creator for his wisdom and power and ask him to break through the hard heart of an atheist or agnostic you know.

nail it down —• Read Genesis 2.

pray about it —•

Confused and concerned, Eileen decides to talk to her science teacher. (Mrs. Dubois's intelligence and willingness to listen make her a favorite with the students.) ▶ After Eileen explains her inner struggle to reconcile the theory of evolution and her belief in creation, Mrs. Dubois points to the *Science Digest* on her desk. "Eileen, I know what you're feeling, believe me. I was brought up in a religious home too. But I came to a point where I had to decide, 'Am I going to base my beliefs on a mythical Bible story, or on the findings of modern science?'"

look it up ⟶ Many advocates of the theory of evolution dismiss the belief in special creation on the grounds that it contradicts science and human reason. Nothing is farther from the truth. God is a God of reason; he gave us his Word to reveal truth, and to lead us into it:

- "'I have not spoken in secret, from somewhere in a land of darkness; . . . I, the LORD, speak the truth; I declare what it is right'" (Isaiah 45:19).

- "Jesus answered, '. . . for this I came into the world, to testify to the truth. Everyone on the side of truth listens to me'" (John 18:37).

think it through ⟶ Some critics label creationism a "religious doctrine" and discount it because it is cited in the Bible. But how does that make a thing untrue? If everything in the Bible is automatically suspect, then we are going to have to rethink morality and ethics. The most basic laws of society are found in the Bible: "Do not murder"; "Do not steal."

We do not have to choose between science and the Bible. It is not science that contradicts God's Word, but *scientism,* the belief that all knowledge must be submitted to the methods of science. The reverse is true: We believe that all knowledge, including scientific knowledge, must be submitted to God's revelation in nature and his Word.

work it out ⟶ Find out if there are any Christians in your community who are experts on the creation/evolution issue. Ask your youth director or Bible study leader to invite them in for a special series on origins.

Practice (with a Christian friend) what you would say if someone called evolution a "fact" (remember, it's still an unproved theory) and creation a "myth."

nail it down ⟶ Read Job 42:2–3.

ileen still has some questions. "Has evolution been proved? Isn't it still just a theory?" In her explanation of the evidence supporting evolution, Mrs. Dubois uses words like *alleles, amino acids, homology,* and *paleobiochemistry.* She concludes, "I think the evidence is pretty clear—every species has evolved from a single living cell that came into existence billions of years ago." "But *how* did it come into existence?" Eileen wants to know.

look it up —• The Bible is not against *micro*evolution—the idea that certain species undergo change. What the Bible refutes is *macro*evolution—the theory that one species can produce an entirely different one:

"And God said, 'Let the land produce living creatures according to their kinds: livestock, creatures that move along the ground, and wild animals, each according to its kind'" (Genesis 1:24; see also 1:11 and 1:21).

"Each according to its kind." In other words, two horses might produce a horse of a different color, but they will never produce anything but horses.

think it through —• Skeptics scoff at the biblical idea of God speaking the universe into being.

"That's absurd! No one can create something from nothing." Yet many of these same scholars are willing to believe that the universe just happened. In other words, they believe *nothing* created *something* out of *nothing!*

work it out —• The best approach to the creation/evolution controversy is not to ignore it or run away from it. Meet the issue head on. Get with a friend and study both views of origins. You may be surprised to find that the "fact" of evolution is constantly undergoing modification and is actually facing serious challenges from within the scientific community.

These books will spark your thinking: *How to Think about Evolution* by L. Duane Thurman; *Evolution: A Theory in Crisis* by Michael Denton; *Evolution: The Fossils Still Say No!* by Duane Gish.

nail it down —• Read Psalm 102:25.

pray about it —•

Origins

91

What Are the Real Facts of Life?

5

or her science term paper, Eileen wrote an essay on "Problems with Evolution: Proofs for Creation." She read tons of material, learned a lot of good things, and came away feeling more confident in her faith. ▶ Mrs. Dubois wasn't wild about the project, but she did say later that some of Eileen's research made her think.

look it up —• Fortunately for us, Jesus spoke clearly on

- The origin of the universe: "God created the world" (Mark 13:19);

- The origin of humanity: "But at the beginning of creation God 'made them male and female'" (Mark 10:6).

Now, either Jesus didn't know what he was talking about, or he was telling a deliberate lie, or he was telling the truth. Those are the only options.

think it through —• Writer Winkie Pratney correctly observed: "We are either: (1) the product of a cosmic crap-game; or (2) engineered by Wisdom, Love, and Power beyond comprehension. . . . These options have

profound implications for the way you feel about yourself and others. What, for instance, do you do when overwhelmed by the beauty and awesome, orderly arrangement of a flower? Vote scenario two and say, 'Thank You, God!' Vote scenario one and be stuck with 'Praise and honor be to Gases, Geology, and Genes.'"

work it out —• Could the marvelous world all around you have happened by chance? Do this experiment:

Print on a sheet of paper this sentence: "Our complex universe came into existence by chance, over a long period of time." Cut the sentence into individual letters and punctuation marks. Put these in a jar and shake them. Dump the letters onto the table. Do they spell anything? Do it several times. Is the result intelligible?

Maybe the characters need to fall for a longer time before they will finally end up in the right combination. Stand on a chair and drop them to the floor. Any luck?

nail it down —• Read Acts 14:15 on Saturday, Hebrews 11:3 on Sunday.

topic

Fear

freedom from f-f-fear

You're in a maze with dozens of passageways. You're not sure where any of them leads. So you take a quick left, then a right. Suddenly you're face-to-face with your biggest fear. ▶ What is it? The future? Rejection? Failure? Death? Disaster? Disease? Something irrational? God? What are the things that frighten you most? ▶ This week we're going to learn how to face those fears head-on. Because life can seem like a maze. And you never know what you might meet around the next corner. ▶ "Do not fear, for I am with you; do not be dismayed, for I am your God. I will strengthen you and help you; I will uphold you with my righteous right hand" (Isaiah 41:10).

Frightened by the Future

A nna stands frozen in the middle of the college fair while all around her students bustle from one booth to the next. ❱ "Why do they make us come to these things?" Anna protests. "I'm only a junior. I don't want to think about college yet. Moving away, living in a dorm with a bunch of strangers, taking hard classes like calculus. . . . I don't want to go! They can't make me go!"

look it up —• Maybe you're like Anna—scared of what lies ahead. If so, you're not alone. Look at Psalm 34. Even David felt fearful and uncertain about the future.

Here's the background of the psalm: David had been anointed as the future king. As a result, jealous King Saul, the reigning monarch, was trying to kill him. Abandoned and terrified, David sat in a cave wondering what the future held (see 1 Samuel 22:1 and 23:10).

Not until David turned to God— "I sought the LORD, and he answered me; he delivered me from all my fears" (Psalm 34:4)— and remembered God's goodness—"Taste and see that the LORD is good; blessed is the man who takes refuge in him" (Psalm 34:8)—was David able to come to grips with his fear.

think it through —• Take a look at the good side of fear: While jogging, you are chased by a vicious dog. Suddenly, you are a world-class sprinter. Covering 100 yards in 10 seconds, you jump a six-foot fence!

Then there's the bad side of fear: Like Anna, you let fear (in this case, fear of the future) paralyze you. You focus on the situation rather than on the solution.

work it out —• Are you afraid of your future? Overwhelmed by the thought of college or career? Scared you won't find happiness? Why not follow David's lead?

1. Seek the Lord. Tell him about your worries and ask him to deliver you from these fears.

2. Remember God's goodness. He's not interested in playing cosmic games with your emotions. The good God who called his creation "good" cares deeply about his people. (Claim the promise of Romans 8:32. It's an amazing verse!)

nail it down —• Read Matthew 6:25–34.

Fear

2 Fear of Failure

ohn unzips his gym bag and removes his sweaty practice uniform. He stares intensely at the words on the shirt, "Collins High Basketball." All of a sudden he's not alone. ❙ "You're not gonna make first team, you know," says Failure. "You don't have a chance. Your dad's really gonna hang his head in shame. Wasn't he all-district?" ❙ "Yeah," says John. ❙ "Face it, dude. Not only will your dad be ver-r-r-y disappointed, but no girl—especially Shannon—wants to go out with a guy who sits on the bench."

look it up —• In Psalm 27 David describes a time when he was surrounded by enemies. He had every reason to feel fearful. He might have been tempted to think, "I'm a failure. See how the people hate me? They've totally rejected me!" But he didn't. Notice his amazing confidence:

"The LORD is my light and my salvation. . . . The LORD is the stronghold of my life. . . . Though an army besiege me, my heart will not fear; though war break out against me, even then will I be confident" (Psalm 27:1, 3).

The implication? "God hasn't rejected me. Therefore, I don't have to be afraid!"

think it through —• A junior named Bob has amazing confidence. He has run for student government, has tried out for several parts in school plays, and has gone out for three athletic teams. He's failed a lot and succeeded a few times. Why is he so fearless?

Because God is the most important person in Bob's life. Bob knows God loves him and will protect him. That knowledge gives Bob the freedom to be bold.

work it out —• Don't let failure bully you around! Let God be your bodyguard and best friend. He loves and accepts you—even if you fail.

This week do something you always wanted to do but have never attempted because of the fear of failure or rejection. Go out for a team, run for an office, call a person you'd like to get to know, interview for a better job. Even if you don't make it, hey, at least you gave it a shot! You haven't lost a thing. And if you do make it, you'll have a great chance to shine for the Lord!

nail it down —• Read Romans 8:38–39.

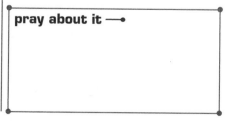

pray about it —•

Fear

When the World Is a Scary Place

Last night the news anchor reported one scary story after another. He talked about the continuing spread of AIDS. He mentioned the fear that some Middle Eastern radicals might have nuclear weapons. ▶ Then he talked about the hole in the ozone layer, the increasing pollution in the oceans, and the new fears of another stock-market collapse. Another report predicted a major earthquake in California. ▶ Today, Candy feels afraid. She thinks, "I don't want to die. I haven't done everything I want to do."

look it up —• Death. Disaster. Disease. Does the Bible give Christians any sort of comfort against these devastating destroyers that strike savagely and suddenly?

You bet.

- "Even though I walk through the valley of the shadow of death, I will fear no evil, for you are with me; your rod and your staff, they comfort me" (Psalm 23:4).

- "God is our refuge and strength, an ever-present help in trouble. Therefore we will not fear, though the earth give way and the mountains fall into the heart of the sea" (Psalm 46:1–2).

- "If calamity comes upon us, whether the sword of judgment, or plague or famine, we ... will cry out to you in our distress, and you will hear us and save us" (2 Chronicles 20:9).

think it through —• Do these verses mean that Christians are exempt from death, disaster, and disease? No. But they do assure us that no matter what we face, God is holding our hand and leading us through to victory.

work it out —• You have two choices today. You can play the "What if?" game—What if I get cancer? What if terrorists attack my city? What if my parents get killed?—and scare yourself silly. Or you can walk with God and trust that he is good enough and powerful enough to do the right thing.

Here's a prayer for everyone who fears any of the three D's: "Lord, sometimes the world is a scary place. You understand that. Help me to not be so fearful. Teach me to focus on you, the Problem Solver, who will one day put an end to all problems, rather than on death, disaster, and disease. Amen."

nail it down —• Read Hebrews 2:14–15.

Fear

4 Look Out for the Phobia Family

More common than people named Smith, the scary members of Phobia family pop up everywhere. Perhaps you recognize some of them. Maybe one of them has even been attacking you. ❭ There's demophobia (fear of crowds); musophobia (fear of mice); belonephobia (fear of needles); astraphobia (fear of lightning); gephyrophobia (fear of crossing a bridge); and about a couple hundred others. There's even one named arachibutyrophobia (the fear of peanut butter sticking to the roof of your mouth)!

look it up —• Are you familiar with any of those characters? More than you'd care to be? Look at Psalm 55.

While not a detailed psychology text about dealing with specific fears, this passage does describe a terribly frightened man—David.

"My heart is in anguish within me.... Fear and trembling have beset me; horror has overwhelmed me. I said, 'Oh, that I had the wings of a dove! I would fly away and be at rest'" (Psalm 55:4–6).

The psalm also shows that David ultimately finds peace. How? By realizing that God hears his cries (vv. 16–17) and by remembering that God is faithful (vv. 22–23).

think it through —• The fears mentioned in the opening story may seem silly to you, but they're no joke to the people who suffer with them.

How would you help someone struggling with one of those fears?

work it out —• Phobias are irrational fears that cause intense hatred of the object of the fear.

Here are some phobias you won't find listed in any psychology textbook:

- Theophobia—the irrational fear and hatred of God

- Christophobia—the irrational fear and hatred of Jesus Christ

- Nomophobia—the irrational fear and hatred of God's law (*Nomos* is the Greek word for law.)

Here's the bad news: Everyone starts out with these phobias (Romans 1:18–32). Here's the good news: Christ can wash them away.

Have you asked Christ to wash your phobias away?

nail it down —• Read Psalm 56:3.

pray about it —•

5 Fearing Your Heavenly Father

ollie's greatest fear? God. ▶ "Sometimes I just get the feeling that he's gonna zap me. I mean, if you read through the Bible, it seems like he's always ticked off at somebody." ▶ Lance, on the other hand, thinks of God as "the Man upstairs." If you ask him, Lance will tell you how glad he is to have a buddy like "the Big G." ▶ Which attitude is right—being scared to death of God, or treating him like a buddy?

look it up —• Neither! Yes, the Bible does say we should fear God. But the fear that believers are to have for God is more like the obedient awe and respect one has for a powerful head of state like a president or a queen, rather than the terror a prisoner of war has for his captor.

"The LORD Almighty is the one you are to regard as holy, he is the one you are to fear, he is the one you are to dread" (Isaiah 8:13).

Such a reverential attitude keeps us from sin (Exodus 20:20), brings blessing in our lives (Proverbs 22:4), and draws us closer to God (Psalm 103:11, 17).

This healthy fear is the result of remembering that one day we will appear before the judgment seat of Christ (2 Corinthians 5:10; Revelation 14:7).

think it through —• If you were to attend a banquet at the White House, would you slap the president on the back? Would you tell a crude joke to Billy Graham? How much more honor does our awesome God deserve?

work it out —• The command to "fear the Lord" means that we approach God humbly, with deep respect and honor.

To develop a healthy fear of God, you need to be a faithful reader of the Bible (Deuteronomy 31:12–13).

To show this fear of God, you need to be a faithful doer of the Bible (Deuteronomy 6:2).

For extra help in learning to fear the Lord, copy Psalm 147:11 on an index card and carry it around with you all day today. It's a great verse!

nail it down —• Read 1 John 4:18. (This verse talks about the wrong kind of fear.) On Saturday, read Psalm 130:3–4. Notice: The right kind of fear follows forgiveness. On Sunday, read Psalm 130:3–4 again—and memorize it.

 **topic**

Authority

the war of independence

ick the statement that doesn't belong:

1. "Get off my back!"
2. "Freedom means doing whatever I want."
3. "Nobody tells me what to do!"
4. "I'll respect and submit to your authority."

In a defiant world, you don't hear that last statement too often. In fact, it's natural to resent and reject the authorities over us, rather than submit to them. ▶ In your own war for independence, declare a truce. Discover that there are alternatives to rebellion. It could be one of the best decisions you'll ever make. ▶ "Humble yourselves before the Lord, and he will lift you up" (James 4:10).

Don't Fight Him; He's on Your Side!

Chuck's family has always been actively involved in church. But about a year ago his mom died in a car wreck. ▶ Now Chuck is extremely bitter. ▶ He says, "My mom really loved God, and look what she got in return. God calls himself loving, but he doesn't even protect the people who follow him. What a joke! I'm telling you, it doesn't pay to try to live for him. From now on, I'm doing whatever I feel like doing."

look it up —• It's understandable that Chuck would be grieving after his loss. But grieving is one thing; judging God is another. Chuck is really saying, "If God does things my way, I'll cooperate. I'll even love him. But as soon as he allows something tragic to happen in my life, I'll no longer do what he says. In fact, I'll hate him."

Chuck's plan will never work.

"'God opposes the proud but gives grace to the humble.' Submit yourselves, then, to God. Resist the devil, and he will flee from you. Come near to God and he will come near to you" (James 4:6–8).

think it through —• If God is the absolute authority in the universe, do you think he's willing to settle for having limited authority in the lives of his children?

People rebel against God's authority for all sorts of reasons, not just when they experience tragedy. Some people who have been blessed with all kinds of good things still reject God's authority in their lives.

Either way, they miss this important truth: God is not a cosmic tyrant who arbitrarily orders people around just for the sake of exercising authority. He's a loving heavenly Father who gives us commands and rules for our own benefit. By submitting, we win, not lose!

work it out —• Have you been rebelling against God in some area of your life? Do you know how to quit fighting that losing battle?

- Admit your pride, asking God to root it out of your life (James 4:6).

- Submit to God, recognizing his lordship in your life (James 4:7).

- Cultivate a closer walk with him to guard against future rebelliousness (James 4:8).

nail it down —• Read Proverbs 29:23.

Authority

The Other Side of Parent Problems

As her date drives away, Chrissy checks her watch—1:15 A.M. She gulps, remembering her dad's words earlier: "Be home by midnight." ▶ "Maybe they're asleep," she thinks. Then her heart sinks. Her dad is at the door. ▶ "Young lady, do you know how much your mother and I have been worrying about you?" ▶ "Good grief, Dad. I'm 17 years old. What's the big deal?" ▶ "Watch your mouth, Chris. As long as you're under our roof, you'll play by our rules. You can forget your plans for the next two weeks."

look it up —• Almost nothing eats at us more than the idea that our parents can boss us around. But look at it from their perspective. God "bosses them around" with regard to how they raise us. He says:

"Train a child in the way he should go, and when he is old he will not turn from it" (Proverbs 22:6).

God expects parents to discipline (Proverbs 23:13), to teach (Deuteronomy 6:6–7), to provide (1 Timothy 5:8).

Whew! No wonder parents are sometimes so uptight!

think it through —• God has instituted several "community units" in his world, each with leaders who are to represent God. Some of these God-ordained community units are the government (Romans 13:1–5), the church (Matthew 16:18–19), the workplace (Ephesians 6:5–9), and (you guessed it) the family (Ephesians 6:1–4).

In all of these community units, people under authority are to submit to their leaders unless their leaders command them to do something forbidden by God, or forbid them to do something commanded by God.

Since God has given your parents authority in your family and also commanded you to submit to their authority, whom are you ultimately rebelling against when you rebel against your parents?

work it out —• Freak your mom and dad out this week by submitting to their authority with no arguments, no discussions. Don't explain your little experiment; just do it until they ask, "Are you feeling okay?"

Besides the fun of seeing their reaction, your obedience will make for better relations on the homefront—and hopefully become your permanent response.

nail it down —• Read Colossians 3:20.

pray about it —•

Showing Class in the Classroom

rs. Barden is a twelfth-grade history teacher who's as tough as nails. In spite of her size (about 5'1") and her age (about 200), she exercises total control in the classroom. ▶ While lecturing on the causes of the Civil War, she is interrupted twice by Keith and Ronnie who are whispering in the corner. ▶ "Okay, guys, that's it. I warned you once. I'll see you both after school in detention hall." ▶ "C'mon, Mrs. Barden, we've got basketball practice." ▶ "Hmmm. I guess you'll be late, won't you?"

look it up ─• Have you ever had a teacher like that? You're tempted to think, "She can't do that!" How does God want you to respond to authority figures at school?

- Submit in order to learn. "Instruct a wise man and he will be wiser still; teach a righteous man and he will add to his learning" (Proverbs 9:9).

- Submit in order to be a witness to non-Christian teachers (Colossians 4:5).

- Submit in order to show respect (1 Peter 2:17).

- Submit in order to be an example to other Christians (Titus 2:7).

As you can see, by submitting you please God, make friends for Christ, and influence others. How can something that does all that be a bad deal?

think it through ─• Sometimes teachers get a little power crazy. Others are unfair on occasion. But humble submission to their authority will always produce better results than a cocky, defiant, rebellious attitude.

Your parents have delegated responsibility to your school. If your teachers represent your parents, and your parents represent God, whom are you ultimately rebelling against if you rebel against your teachers?

work it out ─• If you get along with your teachers, great! Keep working at having good relationships with them by respecting their authority.

If you've had a clash with a teacher, write him or her a short note something like this: "I realize that I acted pretty cocky in your class. Please forgive me for challenging your authority."

Sure, that will be tough. Sometimes it's tough to do what's right.

nail it down ─• Read Proverbs 13:10.

Authority

4 Griping at Government and Cops

look it up —• When that sinking feeling hits your stomach after you see the flashing blue lights in your rear view mirror, you may not be excited to see the officer walking towards your car. And yet the Bible says that Christians must obey and respect all civil authorities.

"Do you want to be free from fear of the one in authority? Then do what is right and he will commend you. For he is God's servant to do you good. But if you do wrong, be afraid, for he does not bear the sword for nothing. He is God's servant, an agent of wrath to bring punishment on the wrongdoer" (Romans 13:3–4).

think it through —• Imagine what would happen if no civil authority existed.

We'd have no defense against foreign invasion. We'd have no system of justice to punish and therefore restrain criminals. People wouldn't bother to take you to court if they had a complaint against you. Instead, they'd just shoot you.

God has instituted civil government and declared rulers to be his servants (or ministers). We are to obey our rulers as his representatives unless they command us to do something God forbids, or forbid us to do something God commands (Acts 4:18–20).

Given those facts, if you unjustifiably rebel against government, against whom are you ultimately rebelling?

work it out —• Thank God right now for civil authority that provides us with safety and security. The alternative is a land where people do whatever they want, whenever they want, to whomever they want.

Resolve to submit to civil authority by following all local, state, and federal regulations that apply to you. You'll please God and avoid a lot of trouble.

nail it down —• Read 1 Peter 2:13–14.

pray about it —•

Authority

5 Don't Forget Who Your Real Boss Is!

alerie works at a fast-food restaurant. It's not the greatest job in the world, but it is nice to have a couple hundred dollars of spending money each month. ▶ The problem? Her boss is giving her the worst time slots and assigning her the grossest responsibilities. She just checked the weekend work schedule and saw that she was closing both nights. ▶ "Valerie," said her friend Melanie, "I'd tell him what he can do with his little schedule."

look it up —• Since slavery was a social institution during his time, Paul discussed principles for master-slave relations. Those same principles are applicable to Christians in today's workforce.

"Obey your earthly masters in everything; and do it, not only when their eye is on you and to win their favor, but with sincerity of heart and reverence for the Lord. Whatever you do, work at it with all your heart, as working for the Lord, not for men, since you know that you will receive an inheritance from the Lord as a reward. It is the Lord Christ you are serving" (Colossians 3:22–24).

think it through —• Imagine the impact Christians could have if they committed themselves to serving their bosses with the same enthusiasm they put into serving God.

Do you realize that God is just as pleased with you when you flip hamburgers to his glory as he is when you sing to his glory in the church choir? We'll be rewarded for our attitude and effort in whatever workplace God places us in.

work it out —• If you're employed as a clerk in a store, be the best clerk you can be. If you throw newspapers, do it as if Jesus Christ were your boss. If you baby-sit, do it with the single purpose of being excellent for the Lord.

Remember, the person who is working strictly for a paycheck has his reward. Work for Christ's kingdom wherever you are, and Christ will reward you (and you'll still get a paycheck).

nail it down —• Read Ephesians 6:5–8. On Saturday, read Psalm 126:5–6. On Sunday, read Saturday's verses again. Have you ever worked so hard for something that you actually cried, only to rejoice when you finally got it?

Authority

Incarnation

When you think of Christmas, the word *Incarnation* probably isn't the first idea that comes to your mind. But when you celebrate Christmas each year, you are actually celebrating the Incarnation of Christ, a truth that was revealed to us by his birth.

Jesus Is God *Incarnate*. God was made into flesh—the same flesh of which we are made. This is one of the most basic doctrines of our faith. It is what makes Christianity different from any other religion. In no other religion does God come to live on earth as a human being. This is why Jesus is called "Immanuel," which in Hebrew means "God with us."

The first person to receive the news of Christ's Incarnation was his mother-to-be, Mary. Since she was a virgin, she did not understand how she could become the mother of Christ, but willingly accepted God's promise that "the holy one to be born will be called the Son of God" (Luke 1:35).

The fact that Jesus' mother was an earthly woman shows that he is human. The fact that she was a virgin shows unmistakably that he is the Son of God. Because he was begotten of God, whereas we are begotten of man, he possesses the Father's divinity.

God did not choose to come to us as some extraterrestrial alien. He had a birth, was raised in a family, and learned how to be a carpenter like his earthly father. He got hungry, got dirty, and went to sleep at night. He felt great love for his friends and great pain when he was betrayed by them. Hebrews 2:18 tells us that Jesus understands and identifies with all of our difficulties in living a life pleasing to God: "Because he himself suffered when he was tempted, he is able to help those who are being tempted."

Just as Jesus is fully human, he is fully divine—fully God. He never left anyone in doubt about this: "I came from the Father and entered the world" (John 16:28). His purpose on earth was to give his life as a payment for our sins that we might be forgiven. And if his life was to be an acceptable payment, it had to be totally free of sin. God knew that no man's life was, or ever would be, free of sin. The only possible way he could save us was to give part of his own life.

We can put our full trust in everything Jesus taught or did because we know he is God. We can know and love him personally as our friend and brother because he is a Man.

That is fantastic news! Have you told anyone lately what the Incarnation means to you?

The Message of the Birds

Despite a godly wife and Christian kids, the middle-aged farmer was skeptical about matters of religion and faith. He had vowed as a young man never to attend church. He had kept that vow for more than 30 years.

So on December 24, the story goes, when the rest of the family headed out into the snow for a special Christmas Eve service, the farmer stayed home.

In a few minutes the man was startled by an irregular bumping sound. Upon investigating he realized the noise was due to a flock of tiny sparrows that were repeatedly flying into the warm room's picture window.

Moved to compassion, the farmer went out into the cold night. He opened the barn door, turned on the building's lights, and left a trail of bread crumbs leading inside. But the birds scattered into the frigid darkness.

The farmer tried other tactics—circling behind the sparrows and attempting to shoo them inside,

whistling at them, going in and out of the house. But nothing worked. The terrified birds couldn't grasp that the man was only trying to help. To them, he was just an alien creature.

In frustration the farmer finally retreated into his house. He watched the doomed sparrows for a long time through the front window. As he pondered their plight, the thought hit him like a bolt of lightning: "If only I could become a bird for just a moment. Then I wouldn't frighten them. Then I could show them the way to safety."

In the next instant, as church bells began chiming in the distance, the farmer was struck by another thought: "Now I understand the faith of my family. This Jesus they love, worship, and serve, was God become man! He took on flesh to offer scared and dying people safety and life."

With tears in his eyes the farmer pulled a dusty Bible off the shelf, sat down in front of the fireplace, and began to read.

Rejection

getting past the pain

Rejection comes in many packages. A dating relationship ends. A home is shattered by separation or divorce. Friends mistreat or ignore one of their own. The bad news is that for many people rejection is a painful fact of life. ▶ Would you like to hear the good news? The Bible has real answers for those who struggle with feelings of rejection. ▶ Discover this week the wonder of God's great love and acceptance! ▶ "In all these things we are more than conquerors through him who loved us" (Romans 8:37).

A Large Order of Acceptance to Go

- Brian is not having a good day. He's new at Adams High School. No one sits by him at lunch. During P.E. class, nobody picks him to participate. In fact, three bigger guys pick on him in front of some girls. Brian feels humiliated.

- Patti is in tears. She just found out that her two closest friends are having a party. They've invited everybody—except her. When she walks to her locker after school, her two "friends" giggle as she passes by.

look it up —• Brian and Patti are going through tough situations. But they're not alone. Every person that ever lived has experienced similar circumstances.

And while it's true that we can't control how others treat us, we can control one thing—how we react.

When you're feeling hurt, these truths can make a big difference:

- Because God created you in his image, he considers you precious and valuable (Genesis 1:26; Psalm 139:13–16).

- God loves you more than you can comprehend (Romans 5:8).

- God is there to care for you even when it seems nobody else is (Matthew 10:29–31).

- God is "the Father of compassion and the God of all comfort, who comforts us in all our troubles, so that we can comfort those in any trouble with the comfort we ourselves have received from God" (2 Corinthians 1:3–4).

think it through —• Regardless of how rejected you may feel, regardless of how unkind others have been, you can know without a doubt that God feels differently about you than those who have rejected you. He'll never be cruel to you or cast you aside. He created you and he's a friend you can depend on.

work it out —• If you're feeling like Brian or Patti for some reason, take a few moments right now to open yourself up to God. Tell him just how you feel.

But don't stop there. Let him tell you about how much you matter to him. Look up the verses above and think about them. Be willing to share what you find with others who feel the bitter pain of rejection.

nail it down —• Read Isaiah 43:1–7.

Rejection

Getting to the Heart of the Matter

I can't believe this, thought Jennifer to herself. *Holly, the weirdest girl at school, is sitting at my lunch table. Will you look at her outfit? Does she wash? She's rambling to me like we're best friends or something. I'm so embarrassed.* ▌Holly's voice trailed off to a whisper. "I know you need to study. But I sat down because I don't know where else to turn. I know you're a Christian, and I've been wondering a lot lately about God and stuff. Can you help me?"

look it up ——• Jennifer swallowed hard as she remembered what she had read that morning in her Bible. "The LORD does not look at the things man looks at. Man looks at the outward appearance, but the LORD looks at the heart" (1 Samuel 16:7).

She had always avoided Holly because of her outward appearance. She would never have guessed that Holly was hungry to know more about God.

A few weeks later, Jennifer said to another friend, "I had Holly figured all wrong. She's different for sure, but really sweet and a lot of fun when you get to know her. And I'm really glad I can share Jesus with her."

When God looks at people, he doesn't see their clothes, their makeup, hairstyles, or reputation. God sees each person's heart. He gets past the superficial stuff to discover what an individual is really about.

think it through ——• Which matters more to you, outer credentials or inner potential?

Looking at others from God's perspective demands that we not reject them for the way they seem on the outside. We must try to get to know them on the inside.

We are responsible to discover the potential in others and encourage them to achieve their best in God's kingdom. Think about it: What a privilege it is to be able to share God's unconditional love with those who have felt the sting of rejection.

work it out ——• Right now think of someone you know who gets rejected because he or she is different. Ask God to grant you the insight to see as he sees—not just external characteristics, but internal character. Then determine to go out of your way to encourage that person.

nail it down ——• Meditate on 1 Chronicles 28:9.

pray about it ——•

Feeling Good about Feeling Bad

wo hours ago, Jim was having a great time at a friend's house. But when the NC-17 movie went into the DVD player, Jim went home. ▶ Jim said to his mom, "Mom, the guys looked at me like I was some kind of freak when I told them I wouldn't feel right seeing that movie." ▶ "That doesn't seem so strange to me," his mom replied. "I wouldn't expect your non-Christian friends to have the same values you do. Why don't you see if a couple of your friends from church would like to come over. I'll order a pizza and you can watch the game on television." ▶ "Thanks, Mom."

look it up —• "If you suffer as a Christian, do not be ashamed, but praise God that you bear that name" (1 Peter 4:16).

As Christians, we are sometimes limited in our relationships with non-Christians. They don't see the world the same way we do; they have a different worldview.

Like Jim, then, we'll sometimes have to make decisions that are unpopular with our friends. As a result, we may feel rejected by those who either can't understand why or don't like the fact that our commitment to Christ comes first.

Many times, though, these feelings of rejection are only in our own minds. Our non-Christian friends often actually respect—rather than reject—us for having the courage to stand up for what we believe.

But even when the rejection is real, we can find comfort in God's nearness (Psalm 34:18) and in his promise to reward our faithfulness to him (Matthew 5:10–12).

think it through —• Are you ever afraid you'll be rejected if you refuse to go along with some of your non-Christian friends' behavior? Do you think if you had been in Jim's shoes you would have done what he did?

It's important to have relationships with unbelievers so that we can be witnesses for Christ. But it is also crucial that we not compromise our convictions just to avoid catching grief from our friends.

work it out —• Try to envision a typical day at school and the different opportunities for either courage or compromise that commonly arise.

Pray for the courage to stand up for what you believe. Then commit your fear of rejection to God.

nail it down —• Memorize Psalm 1:1–3.

Rejection

Recovery from Romantic Rejection

- Jill is devastated. Her boyfriend, Mike, told her that he thought it would be best for them to see other people. Almost immediately he began going out with Missy. Jill feels rejected and depressed. She imagines God is punishing her for something. She also would like to get even with Mike.

- Susan just got "dumped" too. She was really crazy about Randy, but suddenly he quit calling—no explanations, no big breakup scene, nothing! Susan tried to talk to him several times, but he wouldn't give her any reasons.

look it up —• Susan is understandably sad and confused. But she seems to be handling the breakup a lot better than Jill. She doesn't seem to be bitter at God or Randy. She isn't acting like her life is over. And she's actually enjoying dating some other guys.

Here's some good advice: Be like Susan. When a dating relationship ends, remember that

- God is sovereign over all your circumstances, and he is wise in bringing those circumstances to pass: "Will not the Judge of all the earth do right?" (Genesis 18:25);

- God feels for you: "The LORD is gracious and compassionate, . . . good to all; he has compassion on all he has made" (Psalm 145:8–9).

think it through —• The reason Susan was better able to handle her traumatic breakup is because she took refuge in the Lord. That doesn't mean her breakup wasn't painful. But Susan was able to keep her breakup with Randy in proper perspective by reflecting on biblical truths and then putting them into practice—even when she didn't really feel like it.

work it out —• Are you suffering from romantic rejection? Try this prescription:

- Be honest with God about your true feelings.

- Trust God's goodness in the hard times (Psalm 27:13–14).

- Refuse to allow bitterness to spring up in your heart (Colossians 3:12–15).

Take the Master's medicine and see just how much you'll improve. If you have a good friend who's lovesick, share the antidote with him or her.

nail it down —• Read Psalm 30.

pray about it —•

When Rejection Comes Home

5

reg just can't stop thinking about Bill. Last week Bill told him that his parents were thinking about getting a divorce. Today he listened in shock as Bill, who was crying, described his parents' most recent argument: ❱ "I'm sick of all of you. That's why I'm leaving!" ❱ "Fine! Go ahead! But you're not gonna stick me with these kids. I can't control them and you know it!" ❱ "Oh, yeah? Well, if you don't get the kids, you don't get the house!" ❱ Greg didn't know what to say. What in the world can he say or do to help his hurting friend?

look it up —• The next morning as Greg is reading his Bible, he comes across a verse that intrigues him: "All that the Father gives me will come to me, and whoever comes to me I will never drive away" (John 6:37).

"Wow," Greg thinks. "Christ completely accepts us. Hey, that's a verse I need to share with Bill."

think it through —• Greg realizes he can't make Bill's parents act differently. Nor can he really understand what it must be like to live in a home full of conflict, feeling like nobody cares.

But Greg decides to do what he can. He can be a great friend to Bill, providing support and comfort through the rough times. He can share with Bill the love and acceptance that God has for him. And he can pray regularly and fervently for God to work a miracle in Bill's family. In short, Greg can do a lot to minimize Bill's horrible feelings of rejection.

work it out —• Can you relate to what Greg or Bill is facing? Chances are at least one of your friends is going through tough times at home, perhaps feeling rejected and unloved. Ask God to give you the sensitivity to know when your friends are hurting and the wisdom to know what to say.

If you find yourself in Bill's situation, find comfort in the love and acceptance Christ offers. And find a good friend like Greg who will be there when you need him.

nail it down —• Read Psalm 37:5–7. On Saturday and Sunday, read about the most horrible rejection of all time: God's rejection of Christ in our place (Matthew 27).

Rejection

Friendship

how do you measure up?

erhaps you've seen wrinkled old men sitting on a park bench and watched them talk and laugh, endure and enjoy one another, counsel and comfort each other. Is it a mystery? Or is it a miracle? ▶ Friendship. ▶ It's that amazing commitment that means you don't have to put up a front. You can be yourself. You're safe, liked, accepted. ▶ Friendship. ▶ It's more valuable than anything this world has to offer—and more costly. It involves more than doling out a few bucks. You have to give yourself. But you get back more than you ever dreamed. ▶ "Greater love has no one than this, that he lay down his life for his friends" (John 15:13).

Use Your Head to Choose Friends

The Wagners moved to Denver almost eight months ago. ❱ Karen, 14, has yet to make a friend. She sits around watching television and listening to music. She's bored out of her mind. ❱ Sixteen-year-old Helen, on the other hand, has made friends with almost everybody in town. She's always doing stuff, going to parties, and getting asked out. Problem is, she's hanging out with a crowd that is definitely on the wild side. It's to the point that she's seriously hurting her walk with God. ❱ Which of the Wagner girls is in worse shape?

look it up ──• Friendship is more than just finding a group to run around with. In fact, by picking your pals too quickly and without much thought, it's possible to end up with "friends" who really aren't friends after all. This is why the Bible warns us to choose our friends wisely:

"A righteous man is cautious in friendship, but the way of the wicked leads them astray" (Proverbs 12:26).

Another verse points out that "a man of many companions may come to ruin, but there is a friend who sticks closer than a brother" (Proverbs 18:24).

Finally, we are urged to watch out for people who just want to use us (Proverbs 19:6–7).

think it through ──• Think about your circle of friends. How many of those people genuinely care about you? How many of them would stick closer to you than a brother during a crisis? Are any of them using you because of your popularity, money, looks, or abilities?

work it out ──• Let's face it. Christians should have relationships with people who don't know Christ. How else can we be witnesses for him? The problem comes when we let those friendships pull us away from the truth.

If you're involved in a close friendship that's hurting your walk with God, rearrange your priorities. Don't completely walk away from the friendship, but be more cautious. If you're trying to be the best friend to everyone in your whole school, stop and evaluate. Two or three quality friendships are much more valuable than knowing the names of a thousand people.

Here's a prayer for the week: "Lord, I want to learn how to be the best friend I can be. Change me this week as I study what your Word says. Amen."

nail it down ──• Read Deuteronomy 13:6–10.

Friendship

2) Wise Lips Build Strong Friendships

Vance and Mark have been best friends as long as they can remember. As kids they played Little League sports together and were in the same Cub Scout troop. Now they go to the same church and school. ▶ But lately they've drifted apart. Vance feels weird because Mark has started drinking with some rowdy guys on weekends. ▶ And Mark is mad because Vance told some girls at church what is going on. ▶ Sounds like a case of broken-down communication.

look it up —• Good friendships mean that we must communicate with our friends truthfully.

We need to *confront* our friends when they get out of hand: "Better is open rebuke than hidden love. Wounds from a friend can be trusted, but an enemy multiplies kisses" (Proverbs 27:5–6).

In other words, sometimes the truth hurts.

We need to *counsel* our friends when they need direction: "Perfume and incense bring joy to the heart, and the pleasantness of one's friend springs from his earnest counsel" (Proverbs 27:9).

think it through —• Let's play the "Stupid/Smart" game! You decide whether a response is stupid or smart.

• Because of a big fight with her parents, 14-year-old Beth

decides to run away. Her best friend, Tricia, knows Beth is overreacting and is making a big mistake, but she doesn't tell her what she thinks.

• At 6 feet 4 inches, Carl would love to try out for the basketball team. But he's not too confident. He asks his friend Randy what to do, and Randy replies, "How should I know? Do I look like a jock?"

work it out —• Maybe God wants you to confront your straying friends about an attitude or action that needs changing. Ask for wisdom to say the right things. Be careful not to come across with a "I'm-holier-than-you" attitude. If they act mad or hurt at first, that's normal. They'll get over it—if they're really true friends.

You may need to counsel close friends who need direction. Listen carefully and offer solid advice that squares with the wisdom of the Word.

Speaking the truth in love makes strong friendships.

nail it down —• Read Proverbs 28:23.

pray about it —•

Friendship

Friendship Starts in the Heart

Craig is a new Christian who has only been coming to church for a short time. Yesterday he pulled one of the youth leaders aside and said, "I don't know how to say this, but sometimes this place gives me the creeps." ▶ "What do you mean? Why?" ▶ "Well, the girls are always hugging each other every 15 minutes and saying, 'I love you' to their friends. And some of the men go up and hug each other too! If you ask me, it looks gay."

look it up —• One of the best examples of friendship in Scripture is the close relationship between Jonathan and David.

How unlikely! Two brave, battle-hardened warriors. Men of strength and courage . . . and yet, not ashamed to show their love for each other.

In time, a jealous King Saul determined to kill David. In an emotional farewell, Jonathan told his best friend to flee: "Then they kissed each other and wept together—but David wept the most. Jonathan said to David, 'Go in peace, for we have sworn friendship with each other in the name of the LORD'" (1 Samuel 20:41–42).

think it through —• Our culture says "macho" guys shouldn't express emotion. What a warped idea! Expressions of affection don't mean you're strange. They're completely normal! Jonathan and David were two incredibly "macho" men (in a culture where kissing is like our shaking hands) who never gave a second thought to expressing how they felt about one other.

Why can most girls tell each other "I love you" without batting an eyelash? Why can't guys? How come girls are not afraid to get emotional and share their feelings with each other? Why don't guys usually do that?

work it out —• Perhaps right now you can't see yourself saying to your friend, "Hey, I really love and appreciate you." That's okay. At least you can start doing more to show how much you care. What would communicate that message to your friends? Brainstorm a list of things you could say or do to show a friend you care. Then pick something off your list and do it!

nail it down —• Read 1 Samuel 18:1–3.

Friendship

It Takes Guts
and an Iron Will

4

Everybody knows Jason. He's one of the biggest and best players on the football team. He's hilarious. All the members of the "in" crowd at school love to be around him. ❱ Drew is a different story. He's not very athletic or funny or "cool." It's not that people dislike him. They just ignore him. Everyone, that is, except Jason. You can believe it or not, but Jason and Drew are best friends. They go hunting and fishing together all the time and always have a blast.

look it up —• Drew and Jason became friends when they were kids, and they've stayed close even while pursuing different interests. How? Because they understand that true friendship requires that we commit to our friends unconditionally. Consider these wise sayings:

"A friend loves at all times, and a brother is born for adversity" (Proverbs 17:17).

"Do not forsake your friend and the friend of your father, and do not go to your brother's house when disaster strikes you—better a neighbor nearby than a brother far away" (Proverbs 27:10).

Both of these verses stress the importance of commitment in friendship . . . no matter what happens.

think it through —• Commitment means you stick up for a friend when everyone else is trashing him or her. It means you keep in touch. It means you can be counted on when trouble is brewing. It means you don't let minor differences diminish your relationship.

work it out —• Take these steps to become a more committed friend:

- Pray for your friends today and every day.

- Approach a friend with whom you've had a strained relationship lately. Talk about and resolve whatever problem is hampering your friendship.

- Support a friend who is in trouble and who needs someone to believe in him or her. This doesn't mean that you condone the wrong actions, only that you stand with your friend and continue loving no matter what.

- Comfort a friend who is going through a difficult experience. It might not be convenient to go out of your way to help, but that's what commitment requires.

nail it down —• Read Proverbs 27:17.

pray about it —•

The Hands and Feet of Friendship

5

Early on a rainy Monday morning the dreaded phone call finally came. Walt's dad, after a long struggle with lung cancer, died. ▶ While the family huddled together at the hospital, their friends swung into action. People from church brought food, cleaned the house, and volunteered to house out-of-town funeral guests. Walt's two best friends left school to come by and sit with their dazed friend. They didn't say much, but just being there was a huge support.

look it up —• Walt's family was blessed by people who understood the biblical principle that true friendship involves sacrifice.

- "Two are better than one, because they have a good return for their work: If one falls down, his friend can help him up. But pity the man who falls and has no one to help him up!... Though one may be overpowered, two can defend themselves. A cord of three strands is not quickly broken" (Ecclesiastes 4:9–12).

- "Julius, in kindness to Paul, allowed him to go to his friends so they might provide for his needs" (Acts 27:3).

think it through —• This week we've seen the importance of choosing friends wisely with your head, communicating truthfully with your mouth, caring deeply with your heart, committing unconditionally with your will, and, finally today, contributing sacrificially with your hands and feet.

Can your chosen friends count on you for communication, caring, commitment, and sacrifice?

work it out —• Use your hands and feet today to develop deeper friendships. This means action. It means being willing to sacrifice your time, emotion, energy, and even material wealth if necessary for your friends.

Today, use your hands to support friends with pats on the back, hugs, and assistance in doing tasks. Also today, use your feet to walk with friends in times of hurt and to go to whatever lengths are necessary to meet their needs. Go out of your way to help them.

nail it down —• Read 1 Samuel 18:4. On Saturday, read about Christ's model friendship and the way we are to show him our friendship—John 15:13–14. On Sunday, memorize Saturday's passage.

Friendship

 **topic**

Faith

what do you believe?

aith. It's one of those concepts like justice or truth that you perhaps vaguely understand, but find hard to explain to others. ❭ The dictionary says *faith* is "belief not based on proof or evidence." But is that what biblical faith really means? Is it putting your brain on the shelf? Does a believer have to kiss reason and common sense goodbye? ❭ Check out the following pages to learn about the following questions:

- What is biblical faith?
- What common errors or problems hinder true faith?
- How can I increase weak faith?
- Are what I believe (faith) and what I do (works) related?
- How should faith affect my everyday life?

"The righteous will live by his faith" (Habakkuk 2:4).

Figuring Out What Faith Really Is

Here are two speakers at the same youth conference using almost identical words. Are they saying the same thing? ▶ Speaker #1: "Young people, if you want to have your sins forgiven and go to heaven, the Bible says that you need to believe that Jesus Christ died on the cross for your sins and that he rose again. That's what faith is—believing the gospel." ▶ Speaker #2: "Young people, if you want to have your sins forgiven and go to heaven, you need to believe in Jesus. That's what faith is—trusting in the Lord Jesus Christ."

look it up —• Well, is faith believing *that* (agreeing to the facts) or is it believing *in* (trusting in a person)?

- "If you do not believe *that* I am the one I claim to be, you will indeed die in your sins" (John 8:24).

- "For my Father's will is that everyone who looks to the Son and believes *in* him shall have eternal life" (John 6:40).

From just these two verses—we could look at dozens of others—faith appears to consist of both parts: believing the facts about Christ and turning away from our sins and toward him in personal trust.

think it through —• A top-notch repairman finishes working on an elevator on the fiftieth floor of an office building. He then says to the two men watching him, "Climb aboard, guys. She's all fixed up, good as new."

The first man says, "I believe that's an elevator, and I believe you repaired it, but . . . get in? No thanks, I don't trust you enough." The man then takes the stairs.

The second man says to the repairman, "I recognize you. You maintain the elevators in our building, and they always work properly. No problem." He steps inside.

work it out —• Find an index card and write across the top of it "My Faith." Draw a line down the center of the card from top to bottom, making two columns. At the top of the column on the left, write: "Strong." At the top of the column on the right, write: "Weak."

Today, list your acts of strong faith in the "Strong" column and acts of weak faith in the "Weak" column.

At the end of the day, evaluate your faith. Is your faith like the first or the second man's faith? Is your faith strong enough—or too weak—to produce actions?

nail it down —• Read James 2:14–17.

Faith

2) Are All Forms of Faith Okay?

harles says, "I think sincerity is as important as faith. I know a Mormon family whose devotion to God puts mine to shame. Can I look at them and say, 'Your faith is false'? I feel like God is going to say to them, 'Well, at least you were sincere.'"

Cheryl says: "Faith is a pretty shaky deal, don't you think? In other words, you hope all these things about God are true. But you can't know for sure. I mean, after all, you've never seen him."

look it up — When it comes to a subject as crucial as faith, God doesn't want us guessing or relying on our own opinions. Consider these verses:

- "I have declared to both Jews and Greeks that they must turn to God in repentance and have faith in our Lord Jesus" (Acts 20:21). Notice that true faith must be in Jesus, not in sincerity or another religion.

- "Now faith is being sure of what we hope for and certain of what we do not see" (Hebrews 11:1). Notice that faith is not wishful thinking. True faith is "being sure" that what God has said will come to pass.

think it through — Has Cheryl ever seen gravity? No, but she has seen its effects. And so, she has faith that gravity exists. But if invisibility isn't enough to shake Cheryl's faith in gravity, why does it shake her faith in God?

What if Charles's Mormon friend put wings on a tricycle and seriously believed that he could fly it across the Atlantic Ocean? Would he get wet? Obviously. True faith requires more than mere sincerity.

work it out — When you hear your friends saying things like: "All you have to do is be sincere in your beliefs," ask them, "If a person sincerely believed an elephant could fly, would that mean an elephant could truly fly?"

When someone says to you: "Everybody's beliefs are true," ask them, "Does that mean Jesus' belief that he is the only way to heaven [John 14:6] is true?" If they say no, remind them that even they don't really think everybody's beliefs are true. If they say yes, ask them: "Then why don't you put your faith in him?"

nail it down — Read Romans 3:22.

pray about it —

Faith

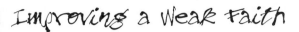

There's a discussion about faith going on in the eleventh-grade religion class at Wesley Academy. Everyone's got something to say (mostly about how little faith they have): ▶ Peggy: "With all the bad stuff going on in my life right now, my faith is just about gone." ▶ Roy: "Yeah, me too. At church we always hear about these missionaries and great men of faith. I can't relate to that! I have a hard enough time just believing in God, much less that he cares about me and wants to 'use me in a powerful way.'"

look it up —• Do doubts attack your faith?

- Time in the Word can make your faith grow. "Consequently, faith comes from hearing the message, and the message is heard through the word of Christ" (Romans 10:17).

- The Lord can strengthen a weak faith (Mark 9:21–27).

- Even a little faith—if it is placed in the person of Christ—can produce powerful results (Luke 17:5–6)!

think it through —• Suppose you were dating someone, but you didn't spend any time with them for a month. Would you still feel confident about the relationship? Probably not. You'd likely begin to wonder what was up. You'd probably be bombarded by doubts.

In the same way, if we're not reading the Bible on a regular basis, hearing what God wants to say to us, we forget his presence, power, and love. We get fearful and our faith begins to crumble.

work it out —• Give your faith muscles a regular workout, beginning today. Be reminded of God's greatness and power by spending a few extra minutes each day in God's Word.

Besides reading the verses that are printed out in the Look It Up sections of this devotional, make sure you look up the Scripture references that are also listed in other sections. And don't forget the additional passages that are mentioned in the Nail It Down sections.

Feeding on the Word of God will build up your spiritual muscles.

nail it down —• Read 2 Thessalonians 1:3.

Faith

4 True Faith Results in Good Works

- In Sunday school or at youth group, Liz can give all the right answers. She can talk about her faith all day and quote Bible verses about the way Christians are supposed to live. But get her away from church, and her lifestyle is anything but Christian.

- Becky, on the other hand, couldn't begin to tell you what she believes! The Bible isn't a book she normally reads, and her church basically just keeps telling her to do good deeds for every-body. So off she goes, working like crazy, trying hard to be a "good Christian."

look it up —• As you probably have already guessed, neither Liz nor Becky's faith is healthy. The Bible is clear on two points:

1. We're saved from sin and death through faith, not deeds. "For it is by grace you have been saved, through faith— and this not from yourselves, it is the gift of God—not by works, so that no one can boast" (Ephesians 2:8–9).

2. Genuine faith results in good deeds. "What good is it, my brothers, if a man claims to have faith but has no deeds? Can such faith save him?" (James 2:14).

think it through —• For centuries, Bible scholars have argued about the connection between faith and good deeds. The whole issue becomes clear when you realize that we are saved by faith alone; however, good deeds are the outcome of real faith. Deeds prove—not produce—saving faith.

Are you like Liz? Like Becky?

work it out —• Does either of these statements describe you: "I'm all talk and no action" or "I'm trying to work my way into heaven"? If so, here's how to find a genuine faith.

First, make sure that you have truly believed. Second, put your faith into practice by doing what God's Word says. Show kindness to a family member or neighbor. Help someone in trouble. Give your time and resources. In short, meet every need that comes your way that you are capable of meeting.

That's what Christ did. And that's what Christians are to do.

nail it down —• Read Hebrews 11 to see how faith is always connected with doing something.

pray about it —•

Faith

5 How Faith Affects Your Everyday Life

All week Amy has been reading about what it really means to believe. She's thought about the connection between faith and good deeds. She probably knows more about what the Bible says about faith than 90 percent of her friends. But still she has some questions. ▶ "It just seems so vague. I know I am saved by faith. But how does faith affect my day-to-day Christian life? Does it really make a difference?"

look it up ⟶ *Does* faith make a difference? Good question! Look at this verse:

"So then, just as you received Christ Jesus as Lord, continue to live in him" (Colossians 2:6).

In essence, Paul is saying this: "You trusted in Christ to forgive your sins and to make you right with God by faith, right? Now, as a Christian, keep on living by faith all the time. Keep taking Christ at his Word. Don't depend on your own power to live the Christian life. And don't depend on your own judgments. Instead, depend on Christ. He lives in you through the Spirit, and he has spoken his judgments to you in his Word."

think it through ⟶ Faith isn't just momentary belief that guaran-

tees heaven and stops at the moment of salvation. And faith isn't a feeling that comes and goes. Faith is recognizing "God said it. I believe it and choose to act on it." Faith means trusting his Word (regardless of circumstances or feelings) and letting him work in and through you in every situation everyday.

work it out ⟶ Want some concrete ways to demonstrate faith? Read on. (And remember, you asked for it!)

Depend on God to give you a love for that person you can't stand, to give you his strength to face a severe trial, to give you a vision and a plan to reach your school for Christ this next year.

Ask God for opportunities to share the gospel, for discipline to meet all your obligations, for new friendships, for growth in your youth group, for a greater hunger for his Word, for creative ways to improve things at home, for a stronger character in your own life. (And believe that he will grant your requests!)

nail it down ⟶ Read 2 Corinthians 5:7. On Saturday read John 15:5. On Sunday read Philippians 2:12–13.

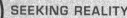

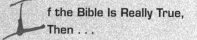

If the Bible Is Really True ...

If the Bible Is Really True, Then . . .

God exists. Belief in a Creator isn't just wishful thinking or the leftover, mythical baggage of our superstitious ancestors. He's for real—holy, eternal, all-powerful, all-knowing, and personal. What's more, he loves you and wants you to know him!

If the Bible Is Really True, Then . . .

Sin is the human race's biggest problem. Sin isn't just a quaint, old-fashioned notion. It is a condition into which everyone is born, and it involves both rebellious attitudes and selfish actions. Sin is what keeps us from knowing God and finding real satisfaction in life. Permeating our lives, sin brings alienation and anguish—and if never dealt with, it leads to an eternity apart from God!

If the Bible Is Really True, Then . . .

Jesus is the answer to our biggest problem. The ultimate solution to our needs isn't found in psychology, sociology, a strong economy, political maneuvering, or a clean environ-

ment. As sinners separated from God, we need forgiveness first and foremost. Only that will bring us back into a right relationship with God.

Through his death on the cross, Christ has provided that forgiveness. It is available. For you. Right now.

If the Bible Is Really True, Then . . .

Real life begins with faith in Christ. It isn't enough to know about God or to occasionally think about his existence. Forgiveness and eternal life are granted when an individual looks at what Christ has done and sincerely says:

"Thank you, Lord, for dying for me. I admit I'm a sinner. Right now, I accept your free gift of salvation. I'm trusting you to fill me with your life and love. Make my life what you want it to be. Amen."

If the Bible Is Really True, Then . . .

You can be a brand-new person inside (2 Corinthians 5:17). What are you waiting for?

Worst Bible Jokes

WARNING! These are unbelievably corny jokes! Tell them only if you want your friends to groan in disgust!

- Who were the shortest guys in the Bible?

  Bildad the Shuhite (shoe height) in Job 2:11; Nehemiah (knee-high-miah) in the book bearing his name. And don't forget the Philippian jailer who fell asleep "on his watch" (Acts 16:27).

- Where is baseball mentioned in the Bible?

  "In the beginning . . ." (The big inning, get it?) (Genesis 1:1).

- Where is tennis mentioned in the Bible?

  "When he saw Queen Esther standing in the court . . ." (Esther 5:2).

- How did the people of Jericho feel after Joshua's armies left town?

  They were crushed.

- Where is basketball mentioned in the Bible?

  "Your basket . . . will be blessed" (Deuteronomy 28:5).

- What is the smallest sin in the Bible?

  "Flee [flea] immorality . . ." (1 Corinthians 6:18 in the New American Standard version of the Bible).

- What did Adam and Eve do after they got kicked out of the Garden of Eden?

  They raised Cain.

- Who was the most wicked man in the Bible?

  Moses. He broke all Ten Commandments at once (Exodus 32:19).

[Have you had enough yet? Only two more . . .]

- Besides Adam, who in the Bible had no parents?

  Joshua was the son of Nun (Exodus 33:11).

- Why were the children of Israel sad when they came out of Egypt?

  They had left their "mummies" behind.

[Aren't you glad that's finally over?]

Character

qualities of a christian

All the students in Mrs. Lansing's second-period English class are writing furiously. ▶ For them, it's an essay on "The Person I Admire Most and Why." For us, it's a chance to examine qualities we need to develop in our own lives. ▶ For them, the goal is simple: a decent grade in English composition. For us, the goal is a little more complex: an A in Character 101. ▶ Sharpen your pencils. ▶ "Be imitators of God" (Ephesians 5:1)

Loyalty

Russell got Mrs. Lansing's assignment mixed up. Instead of writing about a person, he's describing a trait: "Loyalty is what I admire the most in a person. The dictionary says *loyalty* means being faithful to a person, cause, or ideal. It means you can be counted on or depended on. A loyal person is a committed person.

▶ "When I hear the word *loyal*, I immediately think of the firefighters on the scene of the September 11 attack on the World Trade Center. They wouldn't leave as long as they thought there were any survivors in the rubble. If I'm ever in trouble, that's the kind of person I want to help me."

look it up —• Loyalty is a rarity. People change jobs, spouses, churches, and friends without a moment's thought. Is loyalty a character quality Christians should possess? Yes!

Ever heard of Onesiphorus? (How would you like a name like that?) Onesiphorus (we'll call him "O" for short) was a friend of Paul's.

When Paul was in prison for his Christian beliefs, "O" happened on the scene. Most of Paul's friends had deserted him, but not "O"! He risked his own neck (literally!) to come and minister to Paul. The apostle writes in his last letter, "Onesiphorus . . . was not ashamed of my chains. On the contrary, when he was in Rome, he searched hard for me until he found me" (2 Timothy 1:16–17).

Now that's loyalty!

think it through —• Real loyalty survives difficult times. Real loyalty can cost you a lot—your job, your reputation, your friendships, sometimes even your safety or your life.

But doesn't anything really worth having cost a lot?

work it out —• Think of someone in your life who needs a loyal friend right now.

Show your loyalty by

- writing a note;

- paying a visit;

- giving a hug; or

- just listening to your needy friend.

They'll never forget your kindness—or you!

nail it down —• Meditate on John 15:13.

Character

2 How to Run in the Marathon of Life

Jan stared blankly out the window. "I don't know who to write about," she thought. Then as she rubbed a bruise on her knee, an idea came. She began: ▶ "The person I admire most is my aunt Katherine. She's had surgery on both knees about 15 times. Three years ago my uncle Bill died. Now she's all alone. A year ago, she lost one of her legs. ▶ "You'd think all this would make her mad at God. But she still has her faith and she still loves life. She's an amazing woman, my aunt Katherine. I admire her ability to keep at it."

look it up —• Endurance is the ability to hang in there during hard times. It is standing firm under suffering, stress, and trials. Endurance is an admirable trait in anyone, but it's an expected trait in Christians. A good example in the Bible of endurance is in the life of the apostle Paul.

While trying to take the good news of God's love to the world, he was beaten, whipped, imprisoned, shipwrecked, and stoned. He went without food, and sleep (see 2 Corinthians 11:23–27).

But he never quit, because he was aware that God rewards endurance: "Let us not become weary in doing good, for at the proper time we will reap a harvest if we do not give up" (Galatians 6:9).

think it through —• Don't you think there must have been times when Paul felt like throwing in the towel? If you were in a similar situation, do you think you would endure those things for Christ? Why do you think that many Christians, when persecuted or undergoing suffering, seem to get stronger?

There's no magic formula for endurance. Just look to God for his strength and grace and then live by the facts of his Word, not by your feelings (2 Corinthians 5:7).

work it out —• Do you ever feel like quitting because of hard times? Share those struggles with your parents, youth leader, or a close friend. Sometimes, endurance comes easier if we have someone who will walk alongside us.

If you know people who are suffering or hurting, try to help them endure. Think of ways you could help make their rough times a little smoother.

Then do it today!

nail it down —• Read 2 Timothy 2:3.

pray about it —•

3 Compassion

S andra starts writing her essay right away. ▶ "My mom is the greatest lady in the world. I hope I turn out like her. She's a great listener. She trusts me. Plus she likes to do all kinds of fun stuff. ▶ "Most of all, I admire her compassion. If anybody is in trouble, or hurt, she goes way out of her way to help. Once Mom organized the ladies at church to round up clothes and food for tornado victims. And when she sees little kids in wheelchairs, she starts crying! It's kind of embarrassing. But she really cares."

look it up —• For the world's best example of compassion, open your Bible to the Gospels.

Never has anyone been so moved by the needs of people and done so much to meet those needs as Jesus Christ. Look at these examples:

• "When he saw the crowds, he had compassion on them, because they were harassed and helpless, like sheep without a shepherd" (Matthew 9:36).

• "When Jesus ... saw a large crowd, he had compassion on them and healed their sick" (Matthew 14:14).

think it through —• God's goal is that his children become just like Jesus Christ. This means we must ask Jesus to express his compassion in and through us. Our hands and feet become his— and he is then able to use us to show his compassion to a hurting world.

Would Christ make fun of someone who tripped and fell? Would he snicker at a friend in trouble? Would he walk away from anyone who needed and wanted help?

work it out —• Think of some specific ways you could show compassion to the following people:

• a friend who discovers she's pregnant;

• someone who drops his tray in front of 500 people in the lunchroom;

• a person who's being mocked because of the way she looks or dresses;

• a classmate whose parents are splitting up;

• someone who just lost a loved one.

So many people are hurting all around you today. Ask Jesus Christ to minister his compassion through you.

nail it down —• Memorize Colossians 3:12.

Character

4 Be Bold—Break the Mold!

Ricardo has only been in this country for seven years. His family came from Mexico. He's a hardworking, popular student who wants to become a journalist. He writes: ▶ "My hero is Geraldo Rivera. Even though he is a member of a minority, he has become highly successful at what he does. His live documentaries have focused a lot of attention on some of America's biggest problems. ▶ "Geraldo is bold. I don't agree with him all the time, but he's not afraid to confront people with their crimes. I'd like to be that fearless when I become a reporter."

look it up —• The Bible is full of men and women who were bold for God. Take the apostle Peter for instance.

When the first-century church was just coming into existence, Christians faced opposition and persecution from both religious and political leaders. As the leader of the church, Peter might have been tempted to think, "We'd better not rock the boat. We can believe in Jesus, but let's just sort of keep it to ourselves. After all, a person's faith is between him and God."

But he didn't! With a deep faith in God, and empowered by the Holy Spirit, Peter boldly shared the Good News of Jesus Christ with whomever would listen.

And when arrested and ordered to stop witnessing, Peter and John replied, "Judge for yourselves whether it is right in God's sight to obey you rather than God. For we cannot help speaking about what we have seen and heard" (Acts 4:19–20).

think it through —• Boldness doesn't mean being rude or obnoxious. What are some ways a Christian can stand up for Christ without turning everyone off?

Boldness does mean being confident. The better we understand God's love, power, and protection in our lives, the bolder we'll become.

work it out —• Follow these steps for more boldness in your walk with the Lord:

- remember that God is the awesome Lord of all the universe—and therefore in control of your circumstances;

- make sure you're living a life pleasing to God;

- ask God to make you bold. (Since God wants you to be bold, don't you think he'll answer that prayer?)

nail it down —• Read Acts 5:25–29.

pray about it —•

Christi's essay begins like this:

▶ "I look up to a number of people in life. But the person I most respect and admire is my dad.

▶ "My dad is a successful businessman and a leader in the church. He coaches Little League baseball and makes the best blueberry pancakes ever. But if I had to pick one word to describe my dad it would be *dependable.* He's always there for me. If he makes a promise or says he's going to do something, I know I can count on him. How many people do you know who are that reliable?"

look it up —• People respect and seek out people characterized by dependability. The apostle Paul had some dependable friends—the married couple Priscilla and Aquila. Tentmakers by trade, they began to work with Paul in Corinth. As Paul saw how reliable they were, he began to count on them more and more for help in his missionary ventures (Acts 18:18–26).

They were so dependable that when Paul wrote the church in Rome he included this greeting: "Greet Priscilla and Aquila, my fellow workers in Christ Jesus. They risked their lives for me" (Romans 16:3–4).

think it through —• Suppose you've committed yourself to being at a meeting when a friend calls to say he has tickets to see your favorite group in concert that same evening. Or what if you agree to go out with someone, and later a better opportunity arises for you to go out with someone else?

Dependability carries a high price tag. It means that we keep our word no matter what—even if we have to make some unexpected sacrifices.

work it out —• Here's an assignment that will help you be the kind of person that people can count on.

Ask (make) your best friend tell you truthfully whether or not you're a dependable person. If the answer is not what you want to hear, don't attack your friend! Attack the problem.

Begin keeping a schedule book so that you can fulfill all your obligations. Don't commit to more than you can handle. Finally, ask God to make you more reliable.

nail it down —• Meditate on Psalm 15:1–5. This weekend read about one dependable lady—Ruth. Read Ruth 1 on Saturday and reread the same chapter on Sunday.

topic —————————————

Clothes

God's view of chic

When it comes to clothes, how would you describe your attitude? Are you

Satisfied ("11 pairs of jeans is enough.")

Greedy ("I'll take one in every color.")

Guilty ("I can't believe I have a different sweater for each day of the month!")

Indifferent ("Being in style is not a priority for me.")

Jealous ("I hate anyone with great clothes.")

What does God think about clothes? ▶ "Clothe yourselves with the Lord Jesus Christ" (Romans 13:14).

Do You Dress to Impress?

I t's Sunday afternoon and Lisa is looking in her closet in despair. This morning she visited a friend's church where all the girls looked like models and the guys dressed like rock stars. There sat Lisa in her mom's hand-me-down dress. She felt like everyone was staring at her and whispering. Lisa feels sorry for herself. "It's not fair! Why can't I have nicer clothes? I have to dress like a 40-year-old, while they all look hip and cool. I swear, my life would be so much better if I could dress like they do!"

look it up —• Does what you wear impress God? Does he give approval only to those who wear the "right" brands? You be the judge:

- Some people with nice clothes may be destined for trouble: "There was a rich man who was dressed in purple and fine linen. . . . The rich man . . . died and was buried. In hell, where he was in torment, he looked up" (Luke 16:19, 22–23).

- We won't be taking our favorite outfits into eternity with us: "Naked I came from my mother's womb, and naked I will depart" (Job 1:21).

think it through —• How do you feel about these statements?

- Fashion models and designers live happy, problem-free lives because they can wear anything they want.

- Buy a whole new wardrobe for a rapist or drug addict, and he or she will be a new person.

- It's better to spend $50 a month on new clothes than $15 dollars a month to feed a child in Africa.

work it out —• Feeling like Lisa? Take some radical steps:

- Stay out of the malls for a couple of weeks. Hanging out there will only intensify the feeling that everyone but you can afford all the clothes they want.

- Box up your *Seventeen, Sassy, Mademoiselle,* and *Elle* magazines for the time being. The ads and articles in those magazines are designed to convince you to think: "If I want to be 'in,' I need to look and dress like those models."

- Focus on what you do have instead of what you don't. Develop an attitude of thankfulness. Think of all the people in the world who have only one outfit . . . or less!

nail it down —• Read James 2:1–5.

Clothes

2 Pride and Idolatry in the Closet

Lindsay, a great-looking 16-year-old, and her handsome senior boyfriend have been chosen to appear in a fashion show at the mall. ▶ During the show Lindsay carefully arranges her face in a sultry pout—just like the models she sees in *Cosmopolitan*. When she notices several guys from school checking her out, she thinks, *I look pretty hot!* ▶ Meanwhile when a gorgeous college student starts making eyes at Davis, he gets about as puffed up as a blowfish. ▶ In the car on the way home, Lindsay and Davis rave about how great it is to be admired and envied.

look it up ──• Look out! Don't let clothes make you egotistical. Notice what happened when the women of Israel got haughty about their appearance:

"In that day the Lord will snatch away their finery ... the fine robes and the capes and cloaks, the purses and mirrors, and the linen garments and tiaras and shawls. Instead of fragrance there will be a stench; instead of a sash, a rope; instead of well-dressed hair, baldness; instead of fine clothing, sackcloth; instead of beauty, branding" (Isaiah 3:18, 22–24).

think it through ──• There is nothing wrong with wanting to look your best, showing good taste, or enjoying nice clothes. It's fun to express yourself with clothing and develop your own sense of style.

Your *attitude* about clothes is what matters. Ask yourself these questions:

- Do I think about clothes most of the time?
- Does what I have on make me feel important?
- Do I appraise others strictly by what they wear?
- Do all my friends dress exactly the same way?

work it out ──• If you place too much emphasis on clothes or are overly concerned about your wardrobe, pray this:

"God, my attitude about fashion is messed up. I have allowed what I wear to become too important. I'm sorry. Show me how you view clothes. And then help me to get that same perspective this week. Amen."

An experiment for the brave: Wear something really out-of-style to youth group this week. Ask each member to give his or her reaction. It's a great way to open up a discussion on the importance of clothing!

nail it down ──• Read Matthew 23:27.

pray about it ──•

Modesty Is Our Policy

I t looked more like a fashion show at Fredrick's of Hollywood than it did a youth missions trip to the beach. ▶ Some of the girls were wearing teeny string bikinis. When Rick, the youth director, told them to "put some clothes on!" they put on t-shirts that soon became thoroughly wet. ▶ The guys didn't help. They made it clear by which girls they hung around that the way to get attention was to show a lot of skin.

look it up —• The Bible does have something to say about those Christians who make it a habit of running around in seductive clothing:

"I also want women to dress modestly, with decency and propriety, not with braided hair or gold or pearls or expensive clothes, but with good deeds, appropriate for women who profess to worship God" (1 Timothy 2:9).

This verse is addressed to females, but guys need to pay attention as well. If we claim to follow and worship Christ, it is hypocritical to send out sexual messages by the way we dress.

think it through —• Girls, if you could read a guy's mind

when you wear revealing clothes, you'd never wear those outfits again. Do you want to be thought of as an impersonal sex object, lusted over like a piece of meat? Then don't dress like one.

If Christians really care about each other (and God commands us to), we must be willing to stop doing anything and everything that causes a brother or sister in Christ to have wrong thoughts. That includes wearing certain clothes.

work it out —• Are we saying that Christians should dress in ugly, bulky burlap? No! But we are saying that indecent dress is out-of-bounds for believers.

Take a bold step. Girls, ask a mature Christian woman (guys should ask a man) to help you go through your wardrobe and weed out whatever is improper. We're not just talking about swimwear (fashion can be immodest at places other than the beach). What about those tight jeans and sweaters, low-cut dresses, shorts and miniskirts that are too short, tight tank tops, and shirts that expose your midriff, etc.?

nail it down —• Read Proverbs 11:22.

Clothes

4 Dressed Up, Stressed Out

emember Lisa? The girl who felt angry because the girls at her friend's church have expensive clothes? Well, today she feels nervous because she's been invited by some of those girls to a party this weekend. ❯ Her stomach is in knots. "What in the world can I wear?" she asks. "Nothing I have is right! Maybe I could borrow some money from Uncle Frank and go to the mall tonight. I'd rather die than look out of place with those girls."

look it up —• Jesus has a wise word for anxious Lisa (and for everyone else who gets uptight about clothes):

"And why do you worry about clothes? See how the lilies of the field grow. They do not labor or spin. Yet I tell you that not even Solomon in all his splendor was dressed like one of these. If that is how God clothes the grass of the field, which is here today and tomorrow is thrown into the fire, will he not much more clothe you, O you of little faith?" (Matthew 6:28–33).

think it through —• Azalea bushes don't get stressed out about what they look like. They just do what they were created to do—grow and blossom, giving glory to God (Isaiah 44:23).

In the same way our responsibility is simply to do what we were

created to do without comparing ourselves to others—seek first God's kingdom and his righteousness. As we do that God will provide the clothing we need. The real beauty that grows as a flower of love and obedience far outshines anything we can put on our bodies. (More about that tomorrow.)

work it out —• If your constant concern is clothing, not Christ, do these things:

1. The next time you feel an impulse to go out and buy a new outfit, ask yourself whether you really need it.

2. Do not feel sorry for yourself because of clothes you don't have.

3. Stubbornly resist envy of anyone. Remember the Tenth Commandment.

4. Pray about your anxious attitude: "Father, do whatever it takes to cause me to see that clothes are just not worth worrying about. Amen."

nail it down —• Read 1 Timothy 6:8.

pray about it —•

5 The Well-Dressed Soul

You probably have people like Kay and Kent at your school. She's beautiful. He's gorgeous. Since their mother is a buyer for a big department store, they each have a closetful of great clothes. They are voted "Most Beautiful" and "Most Handsome" year after year. ❱ But the problem is that Kay and Kent know they're good-looking, and they let you know it. Hang around them for just a few minutes and their conceited, stuck-up, arrogant personalities will get on your nerves really quick.

look it up —• Suzanne is a bit overweight and she gets her clothes at an outlet store. Yet she's 50 times more popular than Kay. Why are people attracted to her? Because she's fun and interesting and cares about people.

"Your beauty should not come from outward adornment, such as braided hair and the wearing of gold jewelry and fine clothes. Instead, it should be that of your inner self, the unfading beauty of a gentle and quiet spirit, which is of great worth in God's sight" (1 Peter 3:3–4).

Real character will improve your appearance more than the hottest, most expensive fashions in *GQ* or *Glamour*. (And it never goes out of style!)

think it through —• Having a perfect wardrobe and wearing the right clothes will not solve all your problems and make your life perfect. The best-dressed people in your class still fight with their parents, argue with friends, and break up with boyfriends and girlfriends. The real difficulties in your life do not come from a flawed fashion sense but a flawed character.

work it out —• Quit focusing so much on outer appearance and concentrate instead on dressing up your character. Here's some practical help:

- When you get dressed each morning, don't forget to put on Christ (Romans 13:14). To clothe yourself in him means you let others see him at work in your life.

- As you put on your shoes today, tell God that you'll go wherever he sends you.

- If it's still cold where you live, put on your gloves and commit your hands to the Lord's service.

nail it down —• Read Colossians 3:12 on Saturday and 1 Peter 5:5 on Sunday.

Clothes

 **topic**

The Bible

not just any book

*E*veryone has an opinion about the Bible:

- "It's the longest book I've ever seen."
- "Nobody reads our family Bible. It's on a shelf all covered with dust. It weighs about 50 pounds."
- "It's all about God and the miracles he's done."
- "It's full of contradictions. Plus, it's too hard to understand."
- "It's just a bunch of myths and fairy tales."

In this topic, we'll try to answer some of the most common questions people have about the Bible. Maybe you'll find the answer to your question too! ▶ "The grass withers and the flowers fall, but the word of our God stands forever" (Isaiah 40:8).

What's So Great about the Bible?

look it up ⟶• Throughout the entire Bible we find statements like these: "This is what the Lord says" or "the Word was with God and the Word was God." The Bible is God's means of communication with us. In it we can see what our invisible God is like. It reveals his character, discloses his thoughts and plans for planet Earth, and unravels many of life's mysteries.

To answer John, the Bible *is* the greatest book in the world. It is the actual Word of God to humankind:

"And we also thank God continually because, when you received the word of God, which you heard from us, you accepted it not as the word of men, but as it actually is, the word of God, which is at work in you who believe" (1 Thessalonians 2:13).

think it through ⟶• When we watch a beautiful sunset, or think about the complexity of the human body, our thoughts often turn to God. Psalm 19:1–6 agrees that nature reveals much about his glory, power, and ethical standards.

But what if that's all we had to go on? What could we know about God if the only information we had about him was what we see in nature?

He has graciously given us a special revelation of himself—the written Scriptures. Through the Bible we gain a clearer, more complete picture of our Creator.

work it out ⟶• Make this your prayer:

"Lord, help me gain a better understanding and a deeper appreciation for your Word this week. I realize that the Bible is not just another book. It is your revelation to humankind. I recommit myself right now to learning what you have to say to me about my life. Amen."

nail it down ⟶• Compare Hebrews 1:1–2 with John 1:1–2.

As soon as Michael stated that the Bible is God's Word to the world, John launched into this argument: ▶ "Now wait a minute. One minute you talk about the Bible as the Word of God. Then in the very next breath you refer to the psalms of King David, the apostle Paul's letters, the Gospel of John. Those sound like human authors to me. Sorry, but you can't have it both ways. Either the Bible is the Word of God, or it's the writings and opinions of a bunch of men."

look it up —• John's argument sounds logical. The Bible must be either a human or a divine document, right? Not necessarily. It's both human and divine. Consider this:

"All Scripture is God-breathed and is useful for teaching, rebuking, correcting and training in righteousness" (2 Timothy 3:16).

God-breathed means that God is the ultimate author of the Bible. He employed diverse human authors to do the actual writing. But he provided the inspiration, breathing out his Word through human channels.

think it through —• This idea of inspiration, of God "breathing out" the Scriptures, does not mean that he dictated and men merely copied. The human authors crafted the Word of God using their own styles of writing. During this process, they were under the constant supervision and direction of the Holy Spirit.

The fact that the Bible is inspired by God is what makes it the greatest, most important book in existence.

work it out —• Have you read the entire Bible cover to cover? Why not make that commitment right now? Think about it: In just 12 months, you can discover God's written message to the world:

- Find a friend who will take this step with you.

- Get a paperback Bible designed to be read in one year. (You can find one at most Christian bookstores.)

- Pray. Ask God to give you the guidance and understanding you need to approach his Word. He greatly desires to speak to you through the Bible.

nail it down —• Read 2 Peter 1:21.

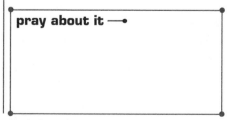

pray about it —•

3 Do We Know the Bible Is Really True?

When Michael insisted that the Bible is the inspired Word of God, John countered with this: "Look, everybody knows the Bible is full of errors and contradictions. Say whatever you want about it being 'breathed out' by God, the fact is the men who wrote it made a lot of mistakes—historically and scientifically. We just can't trust it completely."

look it up —• Actually, we *can* trust the Bible as 100 percent accurate and reliable. Consider this one verse:

"[I am the LORD] ... who says of Cyrus, 'He is my shepherd and will accomplish all that I please; he will say of Jerusalem, "Let it be rebuilt," and of the temple, "Let its foundations be laid"'" (Isaiah 44:28).

This prophecy was given in 700 B.C. About 100 years later Jerusalem was destroyed by the Babylonians. Some 60 years after that, King Cyrus of Persia decreed the rebuilding of Jerusalem— including the temple. A coincidence? Not when you consider that the Bible contains literally hundreds of fulfilled prophecies.

think it through —• Archaeologists have further authenticated the biblical record. Here is another example:

At one time critics rejected the reliability of Luke's Gospel, charging that Quirinius was not governor of Syria at the time of Jesus' birth (Luke 2:1–3). However, an inscription uncovered during an archaeological dig in Antioch has proved Luke's account.

work it out —• Many skeptics try to discredit the reliability of the Bible without really investigating the facts. Such criticism causes some Christians to doubt their faith. Get informed so that you have an answer to such charges.

Two good books to look at are

- *Answers to Tough Questions Skeptics Ask about the Christian Faith* by Josh McDowell and Don Stewart

- *The Case for Christ Student Edition* by Lee Strobel with Jane Vogel

Both discuss many of the so-called contradictions and errors in the Bible. Examine the evidence for yourself and decide whether the Bible really does contain "mistakes." Pick up one of these faith builders and read it this month.

nail it down —• Compare Micah 5:2 with Matthew 2:1.

The Bible

4 Three Steps for Bible Study

Hi, I'm Michael. ▶ "I think it's about time I step in here and show you exactly what I mean. Enough theory about Bible study—let's actually do some! How about starting with this verse: ▶ "'Do not let this Book of the Law depart from your mouth; meditate on it day and night, so that you may be careful to do everything written in it. Then you will be prosperous and successful' (Joshua 1:8)."

Step One: Observation— What Does It Say?

- Read the passage/verse at least two times.
- Write down all the facts and details you observe.

This means you answer questions like: "Who is talking? When is this taking place? What is being said?"

Step Two: Interpretation— What Does It Mean?

Most of the time, the meaning of a passage is easy to see. However, these basic rules help when you read:

- Make sure you know Christ and have his Spirit as your Teacher (1 Corinthians 2:14).
- Let obvious verses help explain obscure ones.
- Make sure you base your experience on the Bible; don't use personal experience to interpret the Bible.

- Don't look for hidden, symbolic meanings when the passage is straightforward.
- Rely on the immediate context of a verse or passage when you need help to determine its meaning.
- Use dictionaries, other translations, commentaries, and Bible concordances to further enhance your study.

Now take five minutes to think about what Joshua 1:8 means.

Step Three: Application— What Must I Do?

When you have correctly observed and interpreted the verse, you must determine the following:

- Is there a command here to obey?
- Is there a sin to avoid?
- Is there a promise to claim?
- Is there an example to follow?
- What must I do in relation to this verse to make its truth a part of my life (James 1:22–25)?

Finally, take two minutes, reflect on Joshua 1:8, and figure out what you need to do.

pray about it —•

The Bible

Does the Bible Make a Difference?

Michael is a good example of the difference the Bible can make in a person's life. ▶ Two years ago, he was your basic shallow Christian. He went to church and avoided smoking, drinking, drugs, and sex. But that negative description pretty much summed up his faith. ▶ Now that Michael is getting into the Word on a regular basis, everyone can see positive things happening in his life. Most exciting of all, he's becoming more and more like Christ. The transformation is slow but steady, and certainly noticeable.

look it up —• Here are just some of the changes the Word has worked in Michael's life:

- Memorizing Scripture has helped him overcome certain temptations. "I have hidden your word in my heart that I might not sin against you" (Psalm 119:11).

- Reading the Bible has caused Michael to grow deeper in his faith (1 Peter 2:2).

- Meditating on God's Word has given Michael direction when he's been faced with big decisions (Psalm 119:105).

- Studying the Bible has equipped Michael to minister to others (2 Timothy 3:17).

think it through —• When all else has faded into oblivion—cars, clothes, parties, schoolwork, money, popularity—God's Word will remain (Matthew 24:35). Does the Bible have its rightful place on your list of priorities?

Why do you think so many Christians in this culture are indifferent about the Bible? What makes believers in oppressed countries willing to risk almost anything to get even a few pages of Scripture?

work it out —• The Bible can truly change your life! Give the Scriptures a chance to work in you.

1. Go back and quickly review the lessons about the Bible in the previous four pages. What truth stands out to you the most?

2. Find a Christian friend and explain why that truth means so much to you today.

3. Set aside fifteen minutes today and read Psalm 119. It's all about the wonderful Word of God.

nail it down —• This weekend, spend some extra time with God and his Word. Read Hebrews 4:12 on Saturday and James 1:22–25 on Sunday.

VIEWPOINT

A Radical Idea

I t's crazy! It's outrageous! It's an idea whose time has arrived.

The idea? *Wearing modest clothing at the beach.*

"Oh, no," you might be thinking. "Here we go again. This guy wants us to wear bathing suits that cover our entire bodies!"

Before you close the book, hear me out.

The Age of Sex: Folks, society is in big trouble. Sexually transmitted diseases are spreading like wildfire. Unfortunately, so is teen sex.

The Atlanta-based Centers for Disease Control (CDC) reported that

- nearly 40 percent of American high school students are currently sexually active;
- nearly 40 percent of ninth-graders and 50 percent of seniors have had sex at least once.

Teens and AIDS: In 2000, 1,688 young people between the ages of 13 and 24 were reported with AIDS in the United States, bringing the cumulative total to 31,293 cases of AIDS in this age group. The CDC estimates that at least half of all new HIV infections in the United States are among people under 25.

Bikini Dipping: Our society provides plenty of stimuli for raging teen hormones. The beach, complete with oiled, scantily clothed bodies, is especially tempting.

Does this mean I'm proposing a beach ban for all Christian teens? Not at all (though given the dangers of premarital sex, that would be a good idea for someone who can't resist temptation at the beach).

But I am proposing this common-sense modesty guideline: If your bathing suit allows someone else to accurately discern at a glance the size and shape of all your body parts, you need to put some clothes on.

New vs. Better: Don't peg me as a prude who "just doesn't understand." When I was a teenager, the so-called new morality was already firmly entrenched. I've experienced both the new morality and the common-sense biblical morality. Take it from me: The biblical morality is better—and safer.

Have fun at the beach. But be modest. Your life might depend on it. That's this editor's viewpoint. Maybe you could see it that way too.

cash It!

Okay, so Jesus never had a checking account. It's doubtful he even had any money. But still, look at all the financial transactions he made on behalf of a bankrupt human race: He purchased Christians with his blood (1 Corinthians 6:19–20; Revelation 5:9).

He paid for the sins of the world (Romans 6:23; John 19:30; 1 John 2:2) with the riches of his grace (Ephesians 1:7).

He forgives our debts (Matthew 6:12).

He reserves treasure in heaven for his faithful followers (Luke 18:22).

To cash this check, all you have to do is believe he died for you and trust him alone to make you acceptable to God.

The check is written and it's signed in blood, so cash it now. With Jesus' impending return, it might be difficult or even impossible to cash it tomorrow! Endorse Christ as your Savior now.

topic ———————————

Prayer

tidying up your prayer life

The **Multiple Misconceptions of Prayer** ▶ "Prayer is like a shopping list you take to God." ▶ "A long blessing at breakfast also covers lunch and dinner." ▶ "Praying with your eyes open doesn't count." ▶ "Prayers said at church are more powerful." ▶ "When all else fails, at least we can pray." ▶ "Lord, teach us to pray" (Luke 11:1).

What Prayer Really Is

Saturday night, Jeannie and Louise have been chattering for an hour when Jeannie finally has to pause for breath: ". . . and did you see who she was with? I almost died," she gasps as her second wind kicks in.

Sunday morning, Jeannie seems like a different person. She sits in her pew with her hands folded, and when the pastor says, "Let us pray," she feels uncomfortable and confused. She thinks, "I feel stupid sitting here when everyone else is praying. What am I supposed to say?"

look it up —• A lot of people can relate to Jeannie. Even long-time Christians freak out at the very thought of prayer. "I can't! I don't know how." Wrong. If you can converse with a friend, you can talk to God. Prayer is simply talking to God. We communicate with our Creator through

- Adoration—praising God for who he is (Psalm 67:3).

- Appreciation—thanking God for the blessings he gives (Psalm 100:4).

- Confession—admitting our sin to God, claiming his forgiveness, and turning away from those wrong attitudes and actions. "I prayed to the LORD my God and confessed: 'O Lord, . . . we have sinned and done wrong'" (Daniel 9:4–5).

- Intercession—asking God to act in the lives of others (Ephesians 6:18).

- Supplication—telling God about our own needs (Philippians 4:6).

think it through —• What are your conversations with God like? Of the five types of prayer listed above, which kind do you do the most? The least?

Would you feel comfortable praying out loud in front of a group? Why or why not?

work it out —• Go to a quiet place and talk to God. Don't worry about phrasing your words perfectly. Just be honest. Pour out your thoughts and feelings. If it helps to talk out loud, do so. If you want to kneel, fine. The important thing to remember is that prayer is simply talking with God. You can do it anytime, anywhere. The point is to do it— today.

nail it down —• Read 1 Chronicles 16:11.

Prayer

How God Reacts to Our Prayers

- Melissa is about to crash for the night. As she kneels beside her bed to pray, these thoughts cross her busy mind: "Why do I even bother? God can't possibly run the whole world, listen to everyone else who must be praying right now, *and* hear me!"

- Tony's feeling anxious about his driving exam, and he'd like to pray about it. But he's afraid to. He imagines God's voice thundering down in a fiery cloud: "How dare you bore me with such trivial matters! Why don't you pray about something important for once!"

look it up —• For those who think that their prayers are insignificant to God, the Bible says, "No way!" Okay, it doesn't exactly say that, but read what it does say.

- God hears and delights in our prayers: "The prayer of the upright pleases him" (Proverbs 15:8).

- God loves to answer prayers: "If you, then, though you are evil, know how to give good gifts to your children, how much more will your Father in heaven give good gifts to those who ask him!" (Matthew 7:11).

- God even helps us pray: "The Spirit helps us in our weakness. We do not know what we ought to pray for, but the Spirit himself intercedes for us with groans that words cannot express" (Romans 8:26).

think it through —• You could think of prayer as a toll-free number to heaven. Call as often as you like. There's no charge, the number always works, and you never get a busy signal or an answering machine.

Have you ever felt like God didn't care? Do today's verses help change your mind? Remember that God is your heavenly Father. He is always concerned about the things that concern you. And because his power is unlimited, you don't have to worry about his not having enough time, or being under pressure.

work it out —• Pray through a section of Scripture. That means you take a Bible passage and say it back to God, putting what you read into your own words. This is a great way to worship God and to get to know him better. The Psalms are especially good for this. (For starters try 103 and 145–50.)

nail it down —• Notice how Christians' prayers are described in Revelation 5:8.

pray about it —•

3 How We Ought to Pray

et's listen in on an episode of *Pathetic Moments in the History of Prayer.* Rich, a laid-back, likable kind of guy (or so he thinks) is attempting to pray: ▶ "So, how's the Man-with-the-plan? How's the King-meister . . . Sorry, I've been a little scarce lately. As a matter of fact, I'm probably gonna be booked up all this month too. So, um, lemme make this quick. Bless everybody (especially me)—that is, if you can hear me. Later."

look it up ➝ Rich gives a pretty good example of what *not* to do. Now here's how we should pray:

- In Jesus' name—Not a magical formula we tack on to the end of our prayers, this means our prayers should be consistent with all that Christ represents (John 14:13–14).

- In faith—"If you believe, you will receive whatever you ask for in prayer" (Matthew 21:22).

- Boldly—"Let us then approach the throne of grace with confidence, so that we may receive mercy and find grace to help us in our time of need" (Hebrews 4:16).

- Continuously—Morning, noon, and night (1 Thessalonians 5:17).

- Reverently—Recognizing the holiness of God (2 Chronicles 20:18).

think it through ➝ How does your own prayer life stack up? If your attitude about prayer is casual, and you feel that—since you're obligated to touch base with God—you might as well get it over with, think some more. You're depriving yourself of the great relationship that God wants to have with you.

work it out ➝ Start your own prayer notebook. This is a fantastic way to develop the habit of prayer . . . plus it gives you a permanent reminder of God's faithfulness!

- Divide each page into two columns.

- Write specific prayer requests (along with the date you first start praying for each item) on the left-hand side of the page.

- When God answers a particular prayer, note the details in the right-hand column.

- Pray for only a few items each day.

nail it down ➝ Note also that prayer must be according to God's will (1 John 5:14–15).

4 · Why Some Prayers Aren't Answered

James is not happy with the way his prayer life is going. First of all, he's been praying for about two months that his parents would change their minds about letting him buy a car. They want him to wait until he is 17, and they have even offered to pay half the cost. But James doesn't want to wait.
▶ Also, James prayed really hard that he would pass the chemistry test he forgot to study for. As he stares at the D- on his paper, he's starting to wonder if God even hears his prayers at all.

look it up —• The Bible lists several reasons why our prayers seem to fall on deaf ears:

- Secret sin—"If I had cherished sin in my heart, the Lord would not have listened" (Psalm 66:18).
- Selfishness—"When you ask, you do not receive, because you ask with wrong motives, that you may spend what you get on your pleasures" (James 4:3).
- A lack of mercy for others (Proverbs 21:13).
- Conflict in the home (1 Peter 3:7).
- An unforgiving spirit (Mark 11:25).
- Doubt (James 1:5–7).

think it through —• What would happen if you took the car without asking, didn't come home by curfew, and then got in a fender bender? Would you expect to walk in and talk with your parents as though nothing had happened? If you asked for an allowance at that moment, would they be likely to meet your request?

Since our parents won't accept an arrangement like that, why do we think we can expect our holy God to agree to such guidelines?

work it out —• Is there anything you can think of that could be hindering your communication with God? Here's a course of action to help you think:

- On a piece of paper, list any situation or thing in your life that you feel God might not be pleased with. (Sometimes writing it down makes it easier to tell.)
- Share your findings with a close friend.
- Ask him or her to pray for you.
- Together try to come up with a plan to remove the barriers that restrict your communication with God.
- Agree to meet daily for prayer during the next week.

nail it down —• Read 1 John 3:21–22.

pray about it —•

5 Can Prayer Really Change Things?

ack Taylor can't believe how his life has changed since he began to pray. ▶ Last year when his family moved to another city, Zack was absolutely miserable. He had no friends, he hated his new school, and he didn't think he'd ever be happy again. In desperation he began to ask God to help him. ▶ Several months later Zack has many new friends; he's discovered that he is a talented basketball player; he leads a youth drama team at his church. But the best thing of all is something Zack didn't even ask for—he has an amazing relationship with God.

look it up ⎯• Zack didn't have to wait until he was desperate to pray, and neither do you. These promises of Jesus ought to get you excited about prayer:

- "I tell you the truth, if you have faith as small as a mustard seed, you can say to this mountain, 'Move from here to there' and it will move. Nothing will be impossible for you" (Matthew 17:20–21).

- "I tell you that if two of you on earth agree about anything you ask for, it will be done for you by my Father in heaven. For where two or three come together in my name, there am I with them" (Matthew 18:19–20).

think it through ⎯• Prayer isn't just desirable—it's essential! God has ordained prayer as the primary means by which his will is accomplished on earth. This explains the old saying, "Satan trembles when he sees the weakest Christian on his knees." It also explains why influential Christians throughout history spent hours each day talking to God.

work it out ⎯• If you've met all the requirements from the previous four pages, you are in a position to see some amazing things. You now have the opportunity to see God move in a powerful way.

Take out your prayer notebook and ask God to do these things:

- Save a lost friend.
- Heal a shattered relationship.
- Draw a straying Christian back to himself.
- Use you in a powerful way.

Then sit back and watch him work!

nail it down ⎯• On Saturday read James 5:16–18. Read Psalm 5 on Sunday morning as a prayer to the Lord.

 topic

Giving

bucks, bank accounts, and the bible

Everybody likes money, but nobody really likes being told what to do with it. ▶ Yet God does just that. He tells us—over and over, throughout the Bible— to give our money away. ▶ That makes some people resentful. Others get self-righteous by adding up how much they give and patting themselves on the back—in public, if possible. But some people have learned the secret of true giving. And they just get blessed. ▶ Want to learn the secret of cheerful giving? Keep reading. ▶ "The Lord Jesus himself said: 'It is more blessed to give than to receive'" (Acts 20:35).

Aren't You Glad God Isn't Selfish?

n September, Abbey was a typical 16-year-old. Her life consisted of school, a part-time job, and involvement in youth group. Then the pretty junior was "discovered" in a mall model search. Suddenly Abbey is flying all over the country, appearing in fashion magazines, and making some big money! ▶ Abbey's modeling career has changed her. She used to be known for her down-to-earth friendliness and generosity. But lately she's become awfully superior and self-centered.

look it up —• You don't have to be a high-priced fashion model to forget two important principles:

- Christians should be thankful for God's amazing generosity. He has showered us with blessings (James 1:17)— including the ultimate gift: "For God so loved the world that he gave his one and only Son, that whoever believes in him shall not perish but have eternal life" (John 3:16).

- We should follow the example of God's generosity. "Be imitators of God ... and live a life of love, just as Christ loved us and gave himself up for us as a fragrant offering and sacrifice to God" (Ephesians 5:1–2).

think it through —• Suppose God had never sent Christ to die for us. Or, imagine how different life would be if he suddenly said, "I'm tired of giving all my stuff to those ungrateful people on Earth. From now on, I'm going to keep all my blessings to myself. No more food or sunlight or rain or answered prayers!"

Aren't you glad our God isn't as selfish as we are?

work it out —• Spend a few minutes thanking God for the spiritual blessings he has given you. Then take time to thank him for the material provisions you enjoy.

End your prayer time by expressing these thoughts:

"Father, you are so generous. I have much more than I could ever need. Work in my life this week so that I become like you in this area. Turn my greed into giving and my selfishness into sacrifice. In Jesus' name, Amen."

nail it down —• Beware of getting so caught up in the gifts that you forget the Giver— Deuteronomy 8:11–18.

Giving

2) Is Your Security in Cash or Christ?

Seventeen-year-old Thomas is a guy who knows what he wants, and how he plans to get it. ▶ "I want to make money—a lot of it. I'm going to major in business, get an MBA from Harvard, then get a job with a Fortune 500 corporation." ▶ Why is his entire plan for the future devoted to making money? ▶ "You've got to have security, for yourself and for your family. You want to make sure their future is rock solid. You can never have too much money in the bank."

look it up —• You *can* put your money in the wrong bank.

"Do not store up for yourselves treasures on earth, where moth and rust destroy, and where thieves break in and steal. But store up for yourselves treasures in heaven, where moth and rust do not destroy, and where thieves do not break in and steal. For where your treasure is, there your heart will be also" (Matthew 6:19–21).

Isn't that ironic? It would seem that money provides security. Yet, the more stuff we accumulate, the more we have to worry about. Plus, these earthly "treasures" gradually steal our affections and get our minds off the things that really do matter.

think it through —• A recent poll revealed that more than 60 percent of college freshmen have

as their number one goal in life "to make a lot of money."

Based on the verses just cited, is that a worthy goal?

In view of the financial setbacks that are possible (being fired, being swindled, being robbed, the collapse of the stock market, runaway inflation, economic depression), is that a secure goal?

work it out —• If you can relate to Thomas's plans, you need to make a difficult spiritual/financial transaction. You need to withdraw your security from the Bank of Wealth and deposit it all in the Bank of God. How?

- Get a concordance and look up every verse in the New Testament that has to do with money or wealth.

- Ask God to do whatever it takes to cause you to put your security in him.

- Begin storing up treasure in heaven by giving money and time to the Lord's work.

nail it down —• Read Matthew 6:25–34.

pray about it —•

Wealth Is There to Share!

3

icky and Caroline are discussing the latest lottery winner—a middle-aged hairdresser from the Midwest who will be getting a check for 1.6 million dollars each of the next 25 years. ❱ "What would it be like to have all that money?" ❱ "I don't know, but I'd sure like to find out—hey, why don't we go right now and buy some lottery tickets?"

look it up —• The desire for wealth that you don't have usually creates one of two problems:

- Frustration: "I can't get it!" "Cast but a glance at riches, and they are gone, for they will surely sprout wings and fly off to the sky like an eagle" (Proverbs 23:5).

- Ruin: "It got me!" "People who want to get rich fall into temptation and a trap and into many foolish and harmful desires that plunge men into ruin and destruction" (1 Timothy 6:9).

You can avoid both kinds of heartache. Decide now that the desire for financial success will never interfere with God's plan for your life—whatever it may be.

think it through —• When someone once asked multimillionaire John D. Rockefeller how much money would satisfy him, he is reported to have replied, "Just a little bit more."

That's how it usually is with those whose chief goal is to accumulate riches. They never feel like they have enough.

work it out —• Forget the lottery. Instead, add up the approximate amount you have spent on yourself in the past month (entertainment, clothes, food, dates, etc.). Next, add up how much you have given to God (offerings and gifts, or contributions to Christian ministries). Which amount is greater?

If your spending is much greater than your giving, try to even things out. At the end of every day, dump all your change into a jar. When the container is full, roll up your coins, cash them in, and give that money to a needy family or a worthy ministry.

nail it down —• Read about the futility of accumulating great earthly wealth—Ecclesiastes 2:20–22; Luke 12:16–21.

Giving

4 Pure Gifts from Pure Hearts

- Sitting with friends during the morning offering at church, Stephen pulls out a crisp $20 bill and makes a big show of dropping it into the plate.
- Benita reluctantly contributes $1 of her $10 allowance. "Great!" she thinks, "now I'll probably run out of money before Friday."
- As the plate comes her way, Clarice reasons, "I'd give my whole paycheck if I was sure God would bless me in return."

look it up —• People give for different reasons:

- Love for God (Luke 7:36–50). A few individuals just want to show their gratitude to God.

- Pride. These people are motivated by the desire to impress others (Matthew 6:1–4).

- Legalism. Others give, not because they want to, but because they feel they have to. "Each man should give what he has decided in his heart to give, not reluctantly or under compulsion, for God loves a cheerful giver" (2 Corinthians 9:7).

- Selfishness. These individuals use verses like Luke 6:38 ("Give, and it will be given to you") to twist the Bible's focus from giving to getting.

think it through —• Generally speaking, those who give do prosper (Proverbs 11:25; Luke 6:38). However, we should view rewards as a *result of,* not the *reason for,* our generosity. Our motives for giving must never become self-serving (Philippians 2:3–6).

The last time you put money in the offering plate or contributed to some charitable cause, what was going through your mind? As best as you can remember, what is the true reason you gave?

work it out —• Here are some giving ideas:

- Mail a Bible to someone in a foreign country.

- Give to a relief organization.

- Collect cans and bottles for recycling and give the money to missions.

- Guard against wrong motives in giving. How? Keep your gifts a secret. (It's also more exciting that way.)

nail it down —• Remember—it's the attitude, not the amount. See Luke 21:1–4.

pray about it —•

"Help me out here," Bridget says. "My family wants to help support this missionary in Spain, but a friend told me that we should first give 10 percent of our income to our church. Then, if we want to give over and above that amount to other people or charities, it's okay. Is that really true?"

look it up ⟶ The New Testament says this about giving:

• Why give? "Freely you have received, freely give" (Matthew 10:8).

• When, who, and how much? "On the first day of every week, each one ... should set aside a sum of money in keeping with his income" (1 Corinthians 16:2).

• How? Willingly (2 Corinthians 8:12); generously (2 Corinthians 9:6); and cheerfully (2 Corinthians 9:7).

• To whom? Christians in need (Romans 12:13); family members (1 Timothy 5:8); widows (1 Timothy 5:16); those who minister God's Word (1 Timothy 5:17).

think it through ⟶ In Old Testament times, Israelites were expected to give, not one, but three tithes—one for the Levites, a second for an annual feast in Jerusalem, and a third for needy individuals. All this was in addition to various freewill offerings!

The New Testament lists no explicit amount, except to say that we should give generously (2 Corinthians 9:6) and in keeping with our incomes (1 Corinthians 16:2).

work it out ⟶ Ten percent is a good starting point, but remember, all money ultimately belongs to God. Practice radical Christianity. In addition to your tithe:

• Take those clothes you've outgrown to an inner-city mission.

• Mail those Christian books you've already read to someone in prison.

• Give some portion of all the money you receive unexpectedly to missions.

• Devote 10 percent of your allowance or earnings to reaching your community for Christ.

nail it down ⟶ On Saturday, read Acts 4:32–35. On Sunday, reflect on Deuteronomy 16:17.

 topic —————————————

Suffering

the point behind the pain

I n the short time it takes you to read this page, the ranks of the suffering will swell by several thousand. ❱ Harsh realities (death, disaster, disease, loss, trouble, violence, hardship, misfortune, calamity, adversity, tragedy, affliction, tribulation, failure) bring harsh results (grief, heartache, depression, agony, disappointment, sorrow, sadness, pain, misery, distress, woe, anguish, despair, hurt). ❱ Are there any answers? ❱ "My comfort in my suffering is this: Your promise preserves my life" (Psalm 119:50).

All over the World, All the Time

One blustery day Barbara sits sipping hot chocolate and listening to her new portable CD player. She thinks about last night: Keith told her he loves her! Things couldn't be better. ▶ Meanwhile, the lives of other teens in the same city are filled with pain.

- Paul's parents are in the middle of a nasty divorce.
- Mike's mom has breast cancer.
- Jan's year-old nephew died last Thursday.
- Beth's father molests her.
- Tim faces major reconstructive surgery after blowing out his knee at football practice.

look it up —• The Bible states that as long as sinful people live in this fallen world, suffering will be a fact of life.

In the Old Testament we are told, "Yet man is born to trouble as surely as sparks fly upward" (Job 5:7).

In the New Testament, Jesus asserted, "In this world you will have trouble" (John 16:33).

think it through —• The question really isn't "Will I suffer?" but "How will I deal with suffering?" Things are going great for Barbara right now, but circumstances can change suddenly. (How is she going to feel next week when Keith dumps her for Missy?)

Which statement describes your feelings right now?

- "Suffering is too unpleasant to even think about."
- "I'm going to pray that I never have to suffer in my whole life."
- "I know serious pain and trouble might afflict me at some point, so I want to learn how to respond in the right way."

work it out —•

- Read today's newspaper or watch a news program on television.
- Make a list of the types of suffering that are reported: deaths, natural disasters, diseases, divorces, etc.
- Make other lists of the suffering you are aware of in your own neighborhood, church, and family.
- Then pray this: "God, the issue of suffering is an ancient puzzle. I know I won't find all the answers this week, but please at least teach me one or two new things that will help me cope, and that will also enable me to be a comfort to others who are in pain. Amen."

nail it down —• Read 1 Thessalonians 3:2–4.

Suffering

aria's father, a policeman, was killed recently during a drug bust. This is how she describes her feelings: ▶ "I know I'm supposed to believe that the Lord is in control and that he loves me. But I feel totally abandoned—like he couldn't care less. When I pray, I feel like I'm just wasting my time. It's like my prayers bounce off the ceiling. And when I try to explain it all to my friends, they just can't understand what I'm going through.

▶ "You tell me—how is my family going to make it? What are we going to do?"

look it up —• Notice how God responded when his chosen people were suffering as slaves in Egypt:

"I have indeed seen the misery of my people in Egypt. I have heard them crying out because of their slave drivers, and I am concerned about their suffering. So I have come down to rescue them from the hand of the Egyptians and to bring them up out of that land into a good and spacious land, a land flowing with milk and honey" (Exodus 3:7–8).

Exodus goes on to show how God used his servant Moses to deliver the people.

think it through —• That passage tells us a lot. It tells us that when God's people are hurting: (1) he sees; (2) he hears; (3) he cares; and (4) he acts.

If you are suffering, be comforted by Exodus 3.

If you know someone who is suffering, be challenged by Exodus 3 to be a Moses in that person's life. How could God use you to help bring comfort to someone who is hurting?

work it out —• Soothe some suffering hearts this week:

- Make personal visits. Telephone calls are okay, and notes are even better. But your physical presence means much more.

- Don't feel the need to offer profound insights or to glibly spout off a bunch of Bible verses they already know. A shoulder to cry on and a listening ear offer more comfort than a lot of talk.

- Don't make people feel guilty for feeling down. If they are sad, be sad with them (Romans 12:15).

nail it down —• Read about the sufferings of the Son of God— Hebrews 5:7–8; 1 Peter 4:1.

pray about it —•

Suffering

The Answer to Why Is Who

look it up —• In the book of Job, Job undergoes an unbeliev-able series of personal tragedies (chapters 1 and 2). Friends offer all sorts of possible reasons why (chapters 3–37), but there is no comfort for Job until God finally speaks (chapters 38–41). Interest-ingly, God never addresses the "why?" question. He simply reveals himself.

Reminded of God's sovereignty, Job responds, "Surely I spoke of things I did not understand, things too wonderful for me to know. . . . My ears had heard of you but now my eyes have seen you" (Job 42:3, 5).

It doesn't take away the pain, but somehow it helps to remember that God is good and that he's in control.

think it through —• An artisan unveils his latest tapestry—a mot-ley colored mass of jumbled and knotted threads. "What's that?" you mumble. The craftsman laughs and flips the ugly textile over revealing a magnificent design. You have been looking at it from the back side!

God's use of suffering in our lives is like that. From where we sit, pain is ugly and useless. But one day we'll see things from a differ-ent perspective. We'll finally understand how he weaves all our sorrow into a wonderful work of art.

work it out —• Go to your church library or to your local Christian bookstore and get a copy of the book *Where Is God When It Hurts?* by Philip Yancey. This award-winning book gives a clear, practical explanation about why there is pain in the world and about how God uses suffer-ing in our lives. It just may prove to be one of the most important books you'll read!

nail it down —• Read Job 13:15–16.

Suffering

4 A New Look at an Old Problem

Two tragedies, two responses: When she was fifteen, Ellen broke her neck in an automobile accident. Paralyzed from the neck down, she has spent the last nine years in a wheelchair. Yet most of the time she is happy and joyful. She has an unusually deep walk with God. People like to be around her. Ten years ago, Carl lost his parents in a plane crash. The initial shock and grief have turned into bitterness over the years. Carl is an alcoholic with no real friends.

look it up —• We see pain and suffering as horrible enemies. Yet the Bible claims that suffering has tremendous value:

- "We also rejoice in our sufferings, because we know that suffering produces perseverance; perseverance, character; and character, hope" (Romans 5:3–4).

- "I consider that our present sufferings are not worth comparing with the glory that will be revealed in us" (Romans 8:18).

Present character. Future glory. How can something that results in so much good be so bad?

think it through —• Consider this poem by an unknown author:

I walked a mile with pleasure;
She chattered all the way,
But left me none the wiser
For all she had to say.
I walked a mile with sorrow;
And ne'er a word said she;
But, O, the things I learned from her
When sorrow walked with me.

work it out —• Here are four proper reactions to pain:

Put yourself in God's hands (Psalm 31:5), remembering that he is good (Psalm 34:8).

Acknowledge that you may never fully understand the reasons for your suffering (Deuteronomy 29:29).

Include sincere thanksgiving (1 Thessalonians 5:18) and rejoicing (James 1:2) in your times of prayer.

Nourish your faith by memorizing appropriate Bible verses on suffering (e.g., 2 Corinthians 4:16–18).

nail it down —• Read Job 23:10.

pray about it —•

Suffering

5 — Choosing Pain over Pleasure

Christopher could have had a dream summer—sleeping late every day and working the coveted afternoon lifeguard shift (excellent rays, lots of girl watching, and decent pay). But he surprised everyone when he said no to the pool job and yes to a missions project in Haiti. ❱ Instead of a pleasure-filled summer of sun and fun, Christopher did back-breaking labor in the most primitive conditions . . . and he wants to go back! ❱ Most people think Christopher is weird. But maybe he's on to something.

look it up —• The life of Moses teaches us about tough choices:

"By faith Moses, when he had grown up, refused to be known as the son of Pharaoh's daughter. He chose to be mistreated along with the people of God rather than to enjoy the pleasures of sin for a short time. He regarded disgrace for the sake of Christ as of greater value than the treasures of Egypt, because he was looking ahead to his reward" (Hebrews 11:24–26).

think it through —• Most people look at all their options and then take the path of least resistance. How many people do you know who are willing to choose a path of pain?

Could you make the tough choice that Christopher made? Had you been in Moses' situation, do you think you could have willingly traded a life of ease for a life of suffering? Why or why not?

work it out —• Make a list of the decisions you'll face in the next few weeks. For instance:

- Will I trade my upcoming weekend of homecoming game celebrations for a retreat with a bunch of junior high kids because my youth pastor needs my leadership?

- Will I stand up for my Christian views on abortion and sex, or will I take the popular, politically correct stance with my peers?

Chances are good that in at least some of those instances, you'll be able to choose an easy road of pleasure or a tough road of pain. Some of your options might even include suffering for being a Christian.

nail it down —• On Saturday read Acts 5:41. On Sunday read 2 Corinthians 6:4–10.

Bible Trivia

Questions:

1. What kind of lights did Noah use on the ark?
2. Who had surgery performed on him while he slept?
3. Which king had the first birthday party in the Bible?
4. Which Old Testament woman bore a child at age 90 and is mentioned more than any other woman in the Bible (56 times)?
5. Who is the only man mentioned in the Bible as being naturally bald?

6. Which American president published an edition of the Gospels that left out all the supernatural elements?
7. What was the "Unrighteous Bible"?
8. In the immensely popular *The Greatest Story Ever Told* (1965), practically every star in Hollywood had a small role. What role, with only one line of dialogue, did legendary actor John Wayne play in this movie about Jesus?

Answers: 1. Flood lights   2. Adam (Genesis 2:21)   3. Pharaoh, at the time Joseph was in Egypt (Genesis 40:20)   4. Sarah   5. Elisha (2 Kings 2:23)   6. Thomas Jefferson   7. An edition, printed at Cambridge in 1653, containing the printer's error, *"Know ye not that the unrighteous shall inherit the kingdom of God?" (1 Corinthians 6:9)*   8. The centurion at Jesus' crucifixion (who said, "Truly, this was the Son of God.")

The above questions have been excerpted from J. Stephen Lang's *The Complete Book of Bible Trivia.* Used by permission of Tyndale House Publishers. All rights reserved.

Miracles

Did Jesus really turn water into wine? Did the Red Sea really divide? For centuries skeptics have claimed that miracles are the superstitious beliefs of pre-scientific people or the psychological aberrations of mentally unstable people. But basically there are two reasons why some individuals reject miracles: intellectual arguments and moral excuses.

Intellectual Arguments

Like the eighteenth-century philosopher David Hume, some people base their argument on the belief that the universe functions according to predictable, unchanging natural laws. Since miracles are by definition an alteration of the laws of nature, and since nature's laws cannot be altered, miracles are therefore impossible.

Faulty Reasoning

But Hume made a big mistake. Natural law is completely uniform *only* if miracles never occur. We who believe in miracles believe nature is uniform—most of the time. But when God, the author of natural law, chooses to operate his universe differently, he can. That's what a miracle is. Miracles are merely God's exceptions to life's general rules.

Moral Excuses

God does perform miracles: he created the universe; he parted the waters of the Red Sea; he raised his Son from the dead. He gives believers new spiritual life. When skeptics say miracles are impossible—regardless of the evidence—they prove that many people will go to great intellectual lengths to suppress the truth they know in their hearts: that God created them and will one day hold them accountable for their actions. In truth, their response is nothing more than an excuse, a moral smoke screen, erected by people who want to be free of their obligation to obey God.

topic ————————————————————————

Motives

a behind-the-scenes look
at behavior

D id you ever feel that someone had a reason for doing something that wasn't completely clear? And you wanted to say: "What are you getting at? . . . What makes you tick? . . . What are you really after?" ▶ Motives. What a fascinating topic. It's one thing to look at how we behave. It's another to try to understand why we act the way we do. ▶ Let's look inside. ▶ "Search me, O God, and know my heart; test me and know my anxious thoughts. See if there is any offensive way in me, and lead me in the way everlasting" (Psalm 139:23–24).

L et's begin our survey of motives with a comparison. Peggy, 17, is a whiz at memorizing Scripture. She tithes on her babysitting money. A Christian since she was five, Peggy has never let cigarettes, alcohol, or drugs even touch her lips. ▶ Brian, 16, accepted Christ about a year ago. No one has ever explained to him how to grow in his new faith. Though he quit smoking pot, Brian still doesn't go to church, but he would if someone invited him. ▶ What do you suppose God thinks about Peggy? About Brian?

look it up —• It's easy to judge people by their actions. But God says it's not just *what* we do, it's *why* we do what we do.

- "All a man's ways seem innocent to him, but motives are weighed by the LORD" (Proverbs 16:2).

- "[The Lord] will bring to light what is hidden in darkness and will expose the motives of men's hearts" (1 Corinthians 4:5).

Our reasons for doing things are just as important, if not more important, than the things themselves.

think it through —• Remember the scribes and Pharisees of Jesus' day? They were ultra-religious. Their behavior was practically flawless. Yet Jesus criticized them more than anyone else (Matthew 6:1–18; 9:3–4). Why?

Because their motives were rotten! They liked being praised and honored. They loved being the center of attention. Basically they were selfish.

Is it possible that Brian (even though he's a new believer in Christ) might have just as pure motives as Peggy? Should we evaluate spirituality *solely* on what a person does?

work it out —• The goal this week is to have God examine our hearts. We want to find out more about why we do the things we do. Ask God for his help:

"Father, I need you this week. I want to do the right things, but I also want to make sure that my motives are pure. Show me where I need to change so that my life can please you even more. Amen."

nail it down —• Read more about motives and the Pharisees—Matthew 15:7–20.

2 You can't Put One over on God

Let's take a behind-the-scenes look at Melinda White's behavior. Like most of us, Melinda is very complex. She has numerous reasons for acting the way she does, and some of those motives are not even clear to her. ❱ One thing about Melinda is that she uses religious activity to enhance her reputation (and to get close to cute guys). She actually believes she's fooling everyone— including God.

look it up —• Though we sometimes act like we can fool God, the Bible says he sees right through our facades.

- Consider the advice given to King Solomon in the Old Testament: "Acknowledge the God of your father, and serve him with wholehearted devotion and with a willing mind, for the LORD searches every heart and understands every motive behind the thoughts" (1 Chronicles 28:9).

- Consider this verse from the New Testament: "Jesus, knowing their evil intent, said, 'You hypocrites, why are you trying to trap me?'" (Matthew 22:18).

You might keep other people from knowing your true motives, but God knows exactly what's in your heart.

think it through —• Are you treating God like he isn't there— like he can't see the real reasons you act the way you do?

God sees right into your heart. He's not impressed when people do the right things for the wrong reasons.

work it out —• Get together today with your best Christian friend. Pray first, asking God for wisdom. Then try to help each other analyze why you do some of the things you do. Discuss the true motives behind your

- dating lives

- involvement in youth group or church

- academic lives

- family interaction

- friendships

Once you have a few answers, bat this question around: "Are those really good reasons for behaving the way I do?"

nail it down —• Read Proverbs 15:11 and Mark 2:8.

pray about it —•

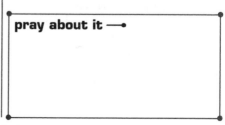

Motives

169

3 Do Totally Pure Motives Exist?

Next we come to Danielle Long, a 15-year-old girl from the Midwest. Last week her Sunday school teacher talked about motives. It was a good lesson that caused the whole class to think. ❚ The problem now is that Danielle is afraid to do anything at all for fear that she might be acting with the wrong motives. Through extreme introspection and constant second-guessing of her every decision and action, Danielle is about to drive herself, and her friends, nuts.

look it up —• It's good to be concerned with having pure motives. (In fact, more Christians should think about why they do what they do.) But it's not good to analyze yourself to death.

Add these twin truths to your thinking about motives:

• As sinful people, we possess impure motives. "The heart is deceitful above all things and beyond cure. Who can understand it? 'I the LORD search the heart and examine the mind'" (Jeremiah 17:9–10).

• As new creations in Christ (2 Corinthians 5:17), we can develop pure motives. "Blessed are the pure in heart, for they will see God" (Matthew 5:8).

think it through —• Have you ever met anyone like Danielle? Are you like her?

Relax! You'll never reach perfection in this world. The point of the Christian life is growth—letting God control more and more of your attitudes and motives. As John the Baptist said, "He must become greater; I must become less" (John 3:30).

The more you learn to do that, the purer your heart will become.

work it out —• Open your Bible to 1 Corinthians 13:4–8. Read the verses out loud, substituting your name every time the word *love* appears.

If the exercise makes you feel uncomfortable (because you know your motives aren't that pure), that's okay. Just pray and ask God to begin working in your heart. Ask him to take control and cause real change in your motives.

nail it down —• Read more about having a pure heart— Proverbs 4:20–23.

4 Can You See Yourself Here?

he Motive Watcher's Almanac might read something like this: "Researchers have thus far cataloged over 143,789 possible impure motives." ❱ You would no doubt be impressed with such an amazing statistic. And, reading on, you might learn that: ❱ "For the sake of simplicity, all the various motives have been categorized under five main headings: anger, jealousy, ambition (or selfishness), pride, and greed."

look it up —• The statistics are right. Bad behavior almost always stems from one of five wrong reasons. Here's what the Bible says about acting out of

- Anger—"Refrain from anger and turn from wrath" (Psalm 37:8).

- Jealousy—"A heart at peace gives life to the body, but envy rots the bones" (Proverbs 14:30).

- Ambition (or selfishness)— "Nobody should seek his own good, but the good of others" (1 Corinthians 10:24).

- Pride—"When pride comes, then comes disgrace, but with humility comes wisdom" (Proverbs 11:2).

- Greed—"The love of money is a root of all kinds of evil. Some people, eager for money, have wandered from the faith and pierced themselves with many griefs" (1 Timothy 6:10).

think it through —• Do you react to family members out of anger or to friends out of jealousy? Is your primary concern to make yourself look better than others?

work it out —• Think before acting. In each instance,

- look at your options. "I can either buy this shirt or not buy it."

- analyze the motives behind each possibility. "If I buy it, is it out of greed or to make someone jealous or to flaunt my physique? If I don't buy it, will I be proud because I have denied myself?"

- ask God to show you the best choice to make.

- choose the option that you feel best about.

- keep renewing your mind daily (Romans 12:2) so God's motives will become your own!

nail it down —• Read about impure motives in prayer— James 4:3.

pray about it —•

Motives   171

W e've learned a lot of things about motives this week, and it must be confessed, the picture so far is pretty depressing. ▶ Wouldn't it be great if we could just zap our bad motives? ▶ Picture, if you will, a gleaming contraption that looks like a helicopter cockpit with hundreds of wires coming out of it. Behind it are large, smoking containers. ▶ This is the amazing "Motivation Modification Machine." All you have to do is step inside and all your impure motives will be changed into pure ones . . . forever!

look it up —• Seeing your motives change is a long, difficult process. Yet there is hope. Note these verses that give us insight into the pure motives and desires of King David:

- "One thing I ask of the LORD, this is what I seek: that I may dwell in the house of the LORD all the days of my life, to gaze upon the beauty of the LORD and to seek him in his temple" (Psalm 27:4).

- "I desire to do your will, O my God; your law is within my heart" (Psalm 40:8).

think it through —• Was David perfect? Did he always have the right motives? Obviously not. He battled (and yielded to) sinful

desires just like we all do. However, during the times he diligently sought to know God and whenever he regularly meditated on God's Word, his motives were (by and large) pleasing to the Lord.

Are you spending time with God daily? Do you let his Word shape your inner thoughts and attitudes?

work it out —• There aren't any shortcuts to having a life that is driven by right motives. Developing a pure heart is something that you will always need to work on.

Start today by getting back to basics:

- Try to memorize a couple of Bible verses each week (and spend time daily meditating on the verses).

- Hang around other Christians who desire to have pure motives.

- Pray each day for God to be glorified in your thinking and decision making.

- Take frequent timeouts to ask yourself, "Why am I acting the way I am?"

nail it down —• On Saturday read 1 Thessalonians 2:1–12. On Sunday read Mark 12:28–33.

Commitment

dedication that makes a difference

What if . . . ▶ Eve had said, "Adam, you're a nice guy, but I don't think I could spend the rest of my life with you." ▶ Moses had said, "You people find your own way to the Promised Land. I'm outta here!" ▶ Christopher Columbus had said, "You know, maybe the world is flat. Let's turn around and go back." ▶ What kind of world would we live in? ▶ Commitment means no backing down, no wimping out, no giving up. ▶ That's the kind of dedication that makes a difference. ▶ "Commit your way to the LORD; trust in him" (Psalm 37:5).

1 The Cult of the Uncommitted

Scene 1: ▶ "You can't quit now—the youth musical is only two weeks away!" ▶ "Look, I just decided I don't want to do it." ▶ "But you promised . . . everybody's counting on you!" ▶ "Well, that's too bad because I changed my mind!"

Scene 2: ▶ "Hey, see you at the beach outreach, okay?" ▶ "Uh, Vic, something, er, came up. I can't make it." ▶ "Can't make it!? You told me yesterday you'd be there. I'm counting on you to drive." ▶ "I'm sorry, but something more urgent came up at the last minute."

look it up —• Commitment is a word that has lost its meaning lately. Look at how fickle people are. Job hoppers, church shoppers, spouse swappers—we're always changing our minds.

This erratic pattern even invades our spiritual life. "Sure, I'm committed to Christ!" we say, as we think, "But only as long as it's convenient and comfortable." Hmm. Sounds a lot like the Jewish leaders in John 12.

"At the same time many even among the leaders believed in [Jesus]. But because of the Pharisees they would not confess their faith for fear they would be put out of the synagogue; for they loved praise from men more than praise from God" (John 12:42–43).

think it through —• Commitment means keeping your promises and being true to your word. In the Christian sense, it means doing the will of God—no matter what:

Check where you are in your Christian commitment.

_____ I usually only live for Christ as long as it's convenient, comfortable, and cool. (I don't want to get too radical, or be too weird!)

_____ I honestly try to do what's right regardless of my own feelings, the opinions of others, or how demanding things become.

work it out —• Without God's direct intervention, all the vows and promises and pledges in the world won't mean a thing. To be truly committed, we need the touch of the Holy Spirit in our lives. Pray,

"Father, deepen my commitment this week. Give me a deeper love for you, a more fervent desire to know you, and a greater willingness to obey you. Amen."

nail it down —• Read Solomon's advice to the uncommitted—Ecclesiastes 9:10.

The Danger of Drifting

ast year at this time Lisbeth was fired up for God. She was involved in youth group, talking to all her friends about Christ, and serious about renewing her mind (she had quit seeing R movies, and had begun a Bible memory plan). ❱ Now, look at her. Oh, she's not doing anything outrageous— robbing banks, shooting drugs—but she's not doing much positive either. She makes it to youth group maybe twice a month, she rarely talks about her faith, and she doesn't even know where her Bible is! ❱ What happened?

look it up —• The Bible warns us not to drift from God.

"We must pay more careful attention, therefore, to what we have heard, so that we do not drift away" (Hebrews 2:1).

You need to understand that the idea of "drifting away" doesn't refer to active rebellion. It's not talking about a person who suddenly decides, "I don't want to be committed to God anymore."

No, it's talking about a gradual process. Imagine the boater who carelessly forgets to drop anchor at bedtime. By morning, he has drifted out to sea ... and into trouble. That's what the drifting Christian is like.

think it through —• This question may sting, but here goes: If every other Christian in the world was as committed to Christ as you are right now, how much of an impact would the church be having?

Have you floated away from God? Is your life more like a boat purposely piloted by Christ? Or a piece of driftwood aimlessly bobbing in the surf?

work it out —• Don't let yourself get blown off course!

• First, with Colossians 3 as your map/compass, chart out your present position. (This will help you see if you are drifting.)

• Second, send out an "SOS." (This means asking God in prayer to either rescue you from your drifting, or keep you from drifting.)

• Third, look for a new crew of "sailors" (that is, a group of committed Christians) nearby who can help you keep your life in "ship-shape."

Remember, commitment means fighting against the tide, not going with the flow!

nail it down —• Read Deuteronomy 4:9 and 8:11.

pray about it —•

Do You Suffer from "Heart Disease"?

3

Imagine these situations:

- As he proposes marriage in the moonlight, Stewart grabs Estelle, looks deeply into her eyes and gushes, "I just want you to know that I love you with . . . 60 percent of my heart!"
- Emily turns to Reed and says, "I love you and I'm totally committed to our relationship . . . maybe. No, wait a minute. Let me think about that. Well, I sort of like you. Last Friday, I really was sure, but now I . . ."

How would you feel if someone offered you a relationship like one of these?

look it up —• The Bible often talks about the heart in describing the center of an individual's life, emotions, will, and character. A careful reading of the Word shows that true commitment takes:

- A whole heart—"Love the LORD your God with all your heart" (Deuteronomy 6:5). Committed people hold nothing back. They seek God, obey and serve him, rejoice in him, and thank him with all their hearts.

- A steadfast heart—"My heart is steadfast, O God, my heart is steadfast" (Psalm 57:7). Committed people are steady, solid, and unwavering.

- A pure heart (Psalm 51:10). Committed people confess their sins quickly and move on.

think it through —• Is your heart completely committed to the Lord? That is, are you giving him 100 percent? If not, what areas of your life are not under his control? Why are you reluctant to give him those things?

Does your commitment waver from day to day? What sort of situations cause you to become shaky in your walk with Christ?

work it out —• The Great Physician specializes in healing diseased hearts. First, ask him to search your heart (pray the prayer of Psalm 139:23–24).

Second, get on his diet and exercise program.

- Remove the dangerous "fats" (bad TV shows, nasty videos, violent movies, and raunchy magazines and music) that contribute to spiritual heart disease.

- Exercise your heart regularly— through prayer and talking about your faith.

nail it down —• Read about King Asa's commitment to God— 2 Chronicles 14–15.

Commitment

Are You Thinking of Bailing Out?

He might be lying in bed, but Jon's mind is racing. ❙ Since trusting Christ at the end of August, Jon has been catching heat from the guys in the neighborhood. "Man, you're insane!" "You better not start getting all holy on us, Jon!" ❙ He stares at the Bible on his bedside table. It looks so weird sitting there. He thinks of the youth meeting coming up next week (and his pledge to say a few words). ❙ "What have I done?" he wonders. "And what am I gonna do?" ❙ Jon is facing one of the first tests of his commitment to Christ. What he decides now will affect his entire life.

look it up —• In John 6, Christ was making many of his followers uncomfortable. Their attitude was, "A little bit of this God stuff is okay, but Jesus has gone way overboard!" The result?

"From this time many of his disciples turned back and no longer followed him" (v. 66).

You can almost feel the tension and the uncertainty as Jesus turns and says to the Twelve, "You do not want to leave too, do you?" (v. 67) It's one of the most dramatic moments in the life of Christ.

Thankfully, Simon Peter breaks the silence (and proves his commitment) by responding boldly, "Lord, to whom shall we go? You have the words of eternal life" (v. 68).

think it through —• What do you think would happen if you told God, "Here's my life. I am yours to do with whatever you desire"?

Are you considering backing off on your Christian commitment because things are too hard, too uncertain? Before you do, consider this: Where else in the world do you expect to find real life and fulfillment? Jesus alone has the words of eternal life.

work it out —• Read the booklet *My Heart, Christ's Home.* (Check your church library or local Christian bookstore for this IVP publication.) Afterward, get a friend to read it, and then discuss it together. Encourage each other to remain committed.

Spend a few minutes trying to envision the scene of John 6. Imagine what Jesus must have felt like. Put yourself in the place of one of the disciples.

nail it down —• Consider the strong words of Elijah in 1 Kings 18:20–21.

pray about it —•

commitment 177

on is talking to his Bible study leader. ❯ "Richard, if I'm really going to be a Christian, I mean, I want to really go for it. I don't want to play games." ❯ "That's great, Jon. So what's the problem?" ❯ "I guess I just feel alone. I don't know too many Christians who are that serious about God. Sure would be nice to have a couple of buddies who feel the same way I do, you know?"

- people at school make fun of your faith.

- it means losing a boyfriend or girlfriend.

- it means a drastic change in your social life.

- it means standing alone against the crowd.

Could you be committed in those situations?

look it up —• You'd be hard-pressed to find a better role model for commitment than the apostle Paul.

He talked about commitment. "I consider everything a loss compared to the surpassing greatness of knowing Christ Jesus my Lord, for whose sake I have lost all things" (Philippians 3:8).

He demonstrated commitment. He spent time in prison, was flogged, exposed to death, had been in danger, knew hunger and thirst, went without food, and was cold and naked (2 Corinthians 11:23–27).

Willing to give up everything. Willing to face anything. Now that's commitment!

think it through —• Commitment is caring about and doing the will of God even if

work it out —• Four things will guard your commitment:

- Take time to be alone with God and his Word today and every day.

- Hang around mature believers. (Find a college student or married couple who really love God and see what makes them tick.)

- Make a public commitment to Christ and then ask your friends to hold you accountable.

- Read a chapter from *Fox's Book of Martyrs, Jesus Freaks,* or *Beyond Belief* each time your faith falters.

nail it down —• Think more about commitment this weekend. On Saturday, read the short book of Ruth. On Sunday, consider the words of Jesus in Luke 14:25–35.

No Halfdom in the Kingdom

Think about this: What good is . . .

. . . *half a night out with friends?* ("Oops! Nine o'clock—gotta get home!")

. . . *half a perfect score on a test?* ("Look class! Thelma made a 50 on her quiz!")

. . . *half a TV show?* ("We interrupt this program to bring you live coverage of the city council zoning meeting.")

. . . *half a birthday gift?* ("Here's the CD player you wanted. You'll get the speakers next year.")

. . . *half a kiss* ("Only one lip, please.")

. . . *half a paycheck?* ("You worked hard, Spike—here's your half-pay. We're keeping the other half.")

Not much, you say? You're right. So why do we often give God only *half* a heart?

You want it all, not just half, right? Well, guess what? God feels exactly the same way (Revelation 3:15–16).

It's pretty easy to be a "half Christian"—thinking about God every now and then, and being committed only when you "feel" like it, living for him just when you're around the people from church.

But the result? A half-abundant, half-fulfilling life. And that's a real drag. After all, half of nothing is . . . nothing. So give God your whole life. If you've never trusted Christ to forgive your sins and give you his eternal life, you need to do that right now. Ask him to come in and change your life.

If you're a Christian with a halfway commitment, you need to reevaluate your priorities. Turn over your plans and wishes and dreams to him. Determine to follow him 100 percent of the time, in every situation . . . and then watch him in return give you all the blessings he has for you.

Materialism

We live, as one pop singer put it, in a material world. We are constantly confronted with new items and are told, "You've got to have this." Deep down we think, "If only I could (drive this car, wear those clothes, have that gadget, live in such-and-such a house—take your pick), then I'd be happy." We think and act as though material goods will bring us the satisfaction we long for in life.

Is this the way believers in Christ should live? What does God say about material possessions?

Material Wealth in the Bible. By scanning the pages of Scripture, we find that material possessions are often the result of hard work (Proverbs 12:27). However, Paul carefully pointed out that *"we brought nothing into the world, and we can take nothing out of it"* (1 Timothy 6:7). So, no matter how many possessions we might accumulate we can't take them with us when we die. (That's why you've never seen a hearse pulling a U-Haul to the graveyard!)

Jesus and Materialism. Jesus told his followers to store up treasures in heaven, rather than treasure on earth. His reasoning was clear—worldly wealth is temporal. At worst it can be destroyed or stolen; at best it will decay. By contrast, heavenly treasure is eternal (Matthew 6:19–21) and can never be lost.

Jesus understood that what we value in life will determine our direction in life. When we value earthly things and invest in them, our focus is on the material world. On the other hand, when we concentrate our time, energy, and resources on eternal investments, we are more concerned with the things of God.

So What? Having material goods is not wrong. Some are very necessary to life. However, when we make the accumulation of material things our primary goal in life, we have a problem. We are guilty of idolatry.

As a follower of Christ,

- What possessions matter most to you?
- How would you react if you lost those possessions?
- Are you investing in what can be lost or in what will always last?

"For where your treasure is, there your heart will be also" (Matthew 6:21).

topic

The Church

making yours even better!

Some of the best features of the first-century church surely must have been the deep fellowship, constant prayer, powerful preaching, reverent worship, and total dependence on God. But the early church also had problems. And so do we. ▶ Isn't it great that much of the New Testament was written to show congregations how to overcome their problems? In other words, weak churches can become stronger ones and good ones can get even better. ▶ Jesus replied, "I will build my church, and the gates of Hades will not overcome it" (Matthew 16:18).

Rules, Rules, Rules, and More Rules!

At Community Church, the students have broken up into small groups to discuss today's lesson—what a Christian looks like. Some of the students seem to have strong opinions. ▶ "I think that Christians should only listen to Christian music," said Kristen. ▶ "I agree. And they shouldn't follow the latest trends. That's just being worldly," Dana added. ▶ "If you're really a Christian, you should be wearing Christian T-shirts to school," Kevin chimed in. ▶ Rhonda just rolled her eyes and thought, *I can't believe this.* Later, she angrily reported the episode to a friend. "I'm so sick of Christians making up all these extra rules. If I have to live by everyone's standards, then I'll never be good enough. No matter what I do, it's always wrong to people like that.

look it up —• By emphasizing extra-biblical rules, some believers make the same mistake that the New Testament churches in Galatia made. The result is a joyless lifestyle of bondage rather than a joyful lifestyle of liberty. Such a legalistic attitude prompted Paul to write the following:

- "Are you so foolish? After beginning with the Spirit, are you now trying to attain your goal by human effort?" (Galatians 3:3).

- "It is for freedom that Christ has set us free. Stand firm, then, and do not let yourselves be burdened again by a yoke of slavery" (Galatians 5:1).

- "But if you are led by the Spirit, you are not under law" (Galatians 5:18).

No wonder the book of Galatians is often called the Christian's Declaration of Independence!

think it through —• Freedom in Christ doesn't mean we can go out and do whatever we want— God wants us to be holy. However, true holiness comes only by living in the power of the Holy Spirit, not by trying to follow an impossible list of petty rules and regulations.

In Christ, we find ourselves liberated from the mentality that says, "I have to do these 55 things to be spiritual" and free to say, "My only concern is keeping in step with the Spirit. I'm free to obey God's rules."

work it out —• How can you avoid the trap of legalism?

1. Be an example. Model the holy but liberated lifestyle of walking in the power of the Holy Spirit.

2. Pray that God would change the hearts of legalistic individuals in your congregation.

3. Study the book of Galatians in detail on your own.

nail it down —• Read Galatians 5:13–26.

The Church

Are You Infected by the World?

eff's church is considered the church to be seen in on Sunday morning. All the most wealthy, powerful, and well-known people in town go there. ▶ Each week the parking lot fills up with Mercedes and Jaguars, and the pews overflow with fashionable, well-dressed men and women. Afterwards while the men talk about sports and business, the ladies discuss children and clothes. ▶ Says Jeff: "It's just a big social event—no different from going to the country club. I don't feel like anything spiritual is even going on."

look it up —• Jeff's church needs to heed the warning given to the church of Laodicea:

"I know your deeds, that you are neither cold nor hot. I wish you were either one or the other! So, because you are lukewarm—neither hot nor cold—I am about to spit you out of my mouth. You say, 'I am rich; I have acquired wealth and do not need a thing.' But you do not realize that you are wretched, pitiful, poor, blind and naked. . . . Those whom I love I rebuke and discipline. So be earnest, and repent" (Revelation 3:15–17, 19).

think it through —• If we only go to church to be seen, to socialize, or to flaunt what we have, we've totally missed the point. The church isn't a club for the comfortable—it's a lifeboat for the drowning. Church membership isn't a credential to be listed on our resumes—it's a cause that should be a driving force in our lives.

Is your church involved *in* the world, loving the lost and helping the hurting? Or is your church *of* the world?

work it out —• Sit down with some friends from your youth group and take the following steps:

- Discuss your lifestyles, focusing on the whole issue of worldliness. Ask the question, "Are we having an impact on the world, or is the world having an impact on us?"

- List the worldly things about your own life that need to change.

- Pray for a more spiritual focus, with less emphasis on temporal and material values.

Remember: A congregation will never change until its individual members change.

nail it down —• Read about another worldly church in 1 Corinthians 3:1–3.

pray about it —•

Building Steeples, Not Peoples

n only six years, Marlene's church has grown from a few families meeting in a theater, to 3,000 people with a new facility the size of a mall. Lots of people are being helped. The church's ministry just keeps on growing. ▶ Yet Marlene is disappointed. "Sometimes I feel like a number, like I'm lost in the shuffle. I like the new worship center and my Sunday school class, but my dad hates it all. He says the church is getting to be like a big business."

look it up ⟶ Some churches, because they're doing a lot of good things, grow so big that they lose that spark that got them going in the first place. Here's what Jesus says to them:

"I know your deeds, your hard work and your perseverance. . . . You have persevered and have endured hardships for my name, and have not grown weary. Yet I hold this against you: You have forsaken your first love. Remember the height from which you have fallen! Repent and do the things you did at first. If you do not repent, I will come to you and remove your lampstand from its place" (Revelation 2:2–5).

think it through ⟶ Here's a truth for both individuals and churches: If you do a lot of good things for Christ but forget the main thing—loving him and putting him first—you're just going through the motions.

Is it more important to be concerned with programs or people? With counting the sheep or feeding them? With getting bigger or getting closer to God?

work it out ⟶ If your church or youth group has lost some of its friendliness, don't just sit back and criticize. Be part of the solution instead of part of the problem.

- Rekindle your own love for God. Take a whole evening or afternoon to pray and renew your commitment.

- Reach out to visitors, making it your goal to get to know one new person each week.

- Talk to your youth pastor about a small group ministry. Once-a-week get-togethers provide the chance to get to know a few other people really well. They provide intimacy even in a large congregation.

nail it down ⟶ Read 1 Thessalonians 3:12–13.

When Toleration Is a Bad Situation

4

Robert was shocked when he heard about a man and woman at his church—both regular attenders—who live together but who aren't married. ▶ "I can't believe it!" he told one of the elders. "Hasn't anyone told them that what they're doing is wrong?" ▶ "Robert, I don't personally approve, but who am I to judge other people? Why, we all have sin in our lives, and besides, they're very supportive members of this church."

look it up ⟶ Loving sinners is one thing. Tolerating open sin in the church is quite another. Listen to this stern warning to the Pergamum church, a body with a "too lenient" code of conduct:

"You did not renounce your faith in me.... Nevertheless, I have a few things against you: You have people there who hold to the teaching of Balaam, who taught Balak to entice the Israelites to sin by eating food sacrificed to idols and by committing sexual immorality.... Repent therefore!" (Revelation 2:13–14, 16).

The message? God doesn't compromise when it comes to sin. Neither should his church.

think it through ⟶ Is it ever appropriate to leave one church and join another congregation? Yes, when you discover either one of these danger signs: A pastor who teaches things that openly contradict God's written Word, or an attitude among the body that tolerates wrong beliefs or sinful behavior.

work it out ⟶ As a church member, you not only have the right but the obligation to speak out if you think such a situation might exist in your church. But first,

- ask God for wisdom in what to do;

- discuss the matter with your parents, your Sunday school teacher, or your youth minister.

As long as your motives are pure, as long as you are polite and respectful, you are perfectly justified in challenging church policies and beliefs.

As a teenager, you're not the "church of tomorrow," you're an important part of the church right now.

nail it down ⟶ Read Revelation 2:19–22.

pray about it ⟶

When to Multiply and Not Divide

ary's dad is on the phone with the music minister. It's obvious what's up—another round between the old-time "Millerites" (loyal to the previous pastor, Dr. Miller) and the younger "Ellisites" (loyal to Rev. Ellis, the new minister). ❱ For over a year the church has been plagued by bickering. Everything from the Sunday school schedule to the amount of money to allocate for missions has triggered a dispute. ❱ "What difference does it make?" Cary thinks, rolling his eyes, while his dad discusses what color the new choir robes should be.

look it up —• Is that what Jesus had in mind when he stated, "I will build my church" (Matthew 16:18)? Not at all. Local churches are to be marked by unity, not discord. Notice Paul's charge to the divided church at Philippi:

"Make my joy complete by being like-minded, having the same love, being one in spirit and purpose" (Philippians 2:2).

This plea came about largely because of a disagreement between two women in the congregation. Paul urged them to settle their differences:

"I plead with Euodia and I plead with Syntyche to agree with each other in the Lord" (Philippians 4:2).

think it through —• Is there division and disharmony in your youth group? Why? What's causing the conflict? Are you a part of the problem?

You may not see how the Lord wants to use you to help resolve the situation, but it's clear that he definitely wants it resolved.

work it out —• Don't reject God's concept of the church just because your local congregation has problems. There aren't any perfect churches.

- Pray for unity in your church.

- If you've had a disagreement with someone in the body, go to that person and resolve your differences. Jesus pronounced a special blessing on peacemakers (Matthew 5:9).

- Get the whole youth group involved. You can, under the leadership of the Holy Spirit, bring about positive changes in your church. Go for it!

nail it down —• Read Ephesians 4:3. On Saturday read 1 Corinthians 1:10. On Sunday read 1 Peter 3:8.

The Church

topic ——————————————————————————

Worship

heartbeat of the christian

oes worship count as one of your more familiar and enjoyable experiences? If not, you might think of worship as merely

- a sea of raised hands in a packed church building.
- frowning faces singing somber hymns from the 17th century.
- organ music bouncing off the walls of a huge, empty cathedral.
- people dancing and/or rolling in the aisles.

Go to the next page for a fresh look at a very important topic.

▶ "Declare the praises of him who called you out of darkness into his wonderful light" (1 Peter 2:9).

Giving God the Glory He Deserves

Karen is gushing over with praise for the newest Olympic figure-skating champion: "There's never been a skater like her—she's perfect. I'd give anything to take just one lesson from her!" ▶ Chuck is gushing with praise for Karen: "She's a total babe. And she's crazy about me—she'd do anything for me. I'm serious—I think about her constantly." ▶ Hey, Chuck and Karen, want to go to a praise meeting at church? ▶ "Praise meeting?!" Chuck groans. "Why would we want to do that?"

look it up —• We give out praise all the time, but no one is more worthy of our praise than God. Like the heavenly creatures that John saw in Revelation, we should praise God as

- Our Creator—"'You are worthy, our Lord and God, to receive glory and honor and power, for you created all things, and by your will they were created and have their being'" (Revelation 4:11).

- Our Redeemer—"In a loud voice they sang: 'Worthy is the Lamb, who was slain, to receive power and wealth and wisdom and strength and honor and glory and praise!'" (Revelation 5:12).

The Almighty One gives us both physical and spiritual life ... don't you think he deserves our worship?

think it through —• Worship is not flattering God so that we can get something out of him (Malachi 3:14). It's not an escape from the problems of life (Psalm 73:16–17, 26). And it's not an empty ritual (Matthew 15:8–9).

"Worship," writes one author, "is the believer's response of all that he is—mind, emotions, will, and body—to all that God is and says and does."

Grade yourself (A–F) in the area of worship.

work it out —• Worship isn't an option—it's a command! God deserves it and we need it. If you don't spend time adoring the Lord, your Christian life will be shallow and ineffective. If you do learn to worship, you'll be plugged into the ultimate power source! Plus, you'll learn a lot about joy.

Ask God to teach you what it means to worship this week. And invite a friend to study the subject with you.

nail it down —• Read Revelation 5:13–14.

Worship

2 Worship Is a Way of Life!

Consider these comments from a youth group discussion on worship: ▶ Ann: "I'm more into private worship—I don't like big church meetings." ▶ Dwayne: "I worship God. He knows I love him. Isn't that enough? Why do I have to do anything?" ▶ Ramona: "It gives me the creeps the way some churches get all emotional in their worship services."

look it up —• Now consider what the Bible says:

- Worship is both private (Psalm 63) and public.

- Worship involves attitudes (Psalm 92:4) and actions (Hebrews 13:16).

- Worship involves the head and the heart. "God is spirit, and his worshipers must worship in spirit and in truth" (John 4:24).

think it through —• You can use this devotional guide in one of two ways: (a) as a quick fast-food snack or (b) as an appetizer for a gourmet meal.

People with the first view read hurriedly and don't bother to look up or reflect on the verses. They get only a tiny bit of spiritual nourishment and rarely have a genuine encounter with God. People with the second view take time to linger in God's presence. They come away filled and satisfied because they have truly worshiped.

Which best describes you?

work it out —• Take your Bible and a song or hymn book to a quiet place. Spend at least 30 minutes (you can do it!) worshiping God. Use these incomplete sentences to guide your thoughts:

- My two favorite psalms are _____ and _____ because _____ _____.

- My two favorite songs are _____ and _____ because _____ _____.

- I want to praise you, God, because you are _____ _____.

- I want to thank you, God, for these five blessings: _____, _____, _____, _____, and _____.

Sing softly, kneel if you like, raise your hands if you desire (1 Timothy 2:8). Quietly worship—out of love.

nail it down —• Read Psalm 100.

pray about it —•

Worship

189

3 — The Rich Results of Worship

Youth group A emphasizes good Bible studies and frequent outings. The attendance often exceeds 100. A lot of teens are keeping on track with God as a result of this youth group. ▶ Youth group B does those same things, but it also has a special praise meeting each week. Only about 20 kids show up, but the maturity and commitment in this group seem so much deeper than in youth group A.

look it up —• What is it about worship that makes such a difference?

- Worship pleases God (John 4:23).

- Worship leads to service. "While they were worshiping the Lord and fasting, the Holy Spirit said, 'Set apart for me Barnabas and Saul for the work to which I have called them'" (Acts 13:2). See an additional example of this truth in Isaiah 6.

- Worship transforms us. "And we, who with unveiled faces all reflect the Lord's glory, are being transformed into his likeness with ever-increasing glory" (2 Corinthians 3:18).

What a great promise! The more we worship God, the more we will be changed from the inside out. People will be able see his light radiating from within us.

think it through —• Does God *need* our worship? Not at all. According to Acts 17:25, he is completely self-sufficient. We worship God to give him the glory and honor he deserves ... and so that we might be transformed by living in his presence!

Are we suggesting that Bible studies and outings are wastes of time? By no means. What we are saying is that serious worship should be at the *heart* of every youth program. Is it in yours?

work it out —• Ask your friends who belong to different denominations what their worship services are like. You might even plan to visit various friends' churches this month and witness their worship services.

(This project may give you some excellent opportunities to share your faith with people who, despite going to church, have not yet accepted Christ! Do it!)

nail it down —• Read Psalm 96.

Will goes to a rock concert on Saturday night. And it really is a spectacular show—lasers, explosions, fire and smoke, multicolored lights, a revolving stage, plus some amazing theatrics and stunts by the band. All Will can say (over and over again) is, "These guys are awesome! This concert is excellent!"

▶ Sunday at noon, as the congregation streams out of church, Steve mumbles, "Man, am I ever glad that's over!" Will nods, "No kidding . . . too bad church can't be like last night."

look it up —• Too many Christians fail to worship because they have forgotten what it means to be in awe of the mystery and the majesty of God. Catch the sense of wonder in this prayer of King David:

"When I consider your heavens, the work of your fingers, the moon and the stars, which you have set in place, what is man that you are mindful of him, the son of man that you care for him? . . . O Lord, our Lord, how majestic is your name in all the earth!" (Psalm 8:3–4, 9).

think it through —• We say that a lot of things are awesome—a sports play, a car, a stereo system, a nice-looking member of the opposite sex. But is there anything more awesome than *God?*

Granted, few church services have the "fireworks" of a rock concert, but when was the last time you went into a worship service really expecting God to speak to you? If you were to approach worship with the same attitude of expectation you'd have for, say, a great concert, you'd come out of the service absolutely floored.

work it out —• Some teenagers get to bed so late on Saturday night that they are too tired for church. Too drained to sing or pay attention to the sermon, they complain, "Church is so boring!" The real problem isn't church or the worship service—it's a lack of sleep.

Make the commitment this week to get to bed by 11 P.M. on Saturday night. Have a friend keep you accountable.

Before the service starts, tell God you really want to worship him. Ask him to prepare your heart, and give you a sense of wonder. You won't be disappointed.

nail it down —• Notice the apostle Paul's sense of wonder in Romans 11:33.

pray about it —•

Nature Worships; Do You?

Walt's high school group takes a "One Day Getaway" at the beginning of each summer. It works like this: ❙ The students and leaders leave early in the morning for a nearby park. They spend the morning in individual worship. Some sit by the lake reading their Bibles and praying. Others walk on the mountain trails. ❙ In the afternoon they gather for sharing and praise. Each time, Walt notes the chirping birds and the blooming flowers and says, "Hey, look! We're not the only ones worshiping God today!"

look it up —• Have you ever stopped to think that nature is busy praising God? It's true:

"Praise him, sun and moon, praise him, all you shining stars. Praise him, you highest heavens and you waters above the skies. Let them praise the name of the LORD, for he commanded and they were created. He set them in place for ever and ever; he gave a decree that will never pass away. Praise the LORD from the earth, you great sea creatures and all ocean depths, lightning and hail, snow and clouds, stormy winds that do his bidding, you mountains and all hills, fruit trees and all cedars, wild animals and all cattle, small creatures and flying birds" (Psalm 148:3–10).

think it through —• Match each part of nature to the aspect of God it reminds you of (more than one answer may apply):

___ mountains   a. God's creativity

___ clouds and rain   b. God's humor

___ thunder and lightning   c. God's wisdom

___ rivers and streams   d. God's power

___ giraffes and chimpanzees   e. God's majesty

work it out —• Steal Walt's idea. Go by yourself or with some Christian friends to a quiet park and spend some time with God.

• Reread the verses listed in these pages on worship.

• Reflect on all the ways nature praises him.

• Renew your commitment to be a worshiping Christian. (Begin right where you are by praising God for who he is.)

nail it down —• On Saturday, read Psalm 19:1 and Psalm 96:11–13. In preparation for worship on Sunday, read Psalm 69:34 and Psalm 98:7–9.